HOW TO BE A ~~FANTASTIC~~ ~~SENSATIONAL~~ GOOD ENOUGH KID

ALICE PEEL is a primary school teacher and co-founder of Grow Your Mind, a mental health social venture. She holds a Graduate Diploma of Teaching and Learning from the University of Southern Queensland, a Masters of International Public Health from the University of Sydney and has undertaken courses in positive psychology and neuroscience.

‘I hope every kid gets a copy of this book!’
Dr Addie Wootten, Smiling Mind

‘A life changing book where the reader learns new skills to navigate life’s ups and downs with perspective, resilience and at times joy.’
Lizzy Kirby, Counsellor

‘An important companion for young people trying to make sense of their world, their relationships and themselves.’
Charlotte Board, School Psychologist

‘A gem of a book with loads of practical strategies for young people.’
Karen Young, Anxiety Expert

‘My go-to gift for families, teachers and my recovering perfectionist friends!’
Natalie Hay, Registered Social Worker

GROW YOUR MIND

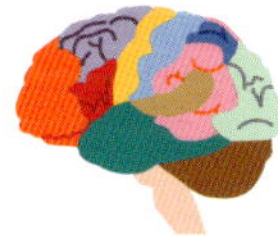

HOW TO BE A ~~FANTASTIC~~ ~~SENSATIONAL~~ GOOD ENOUGH KID

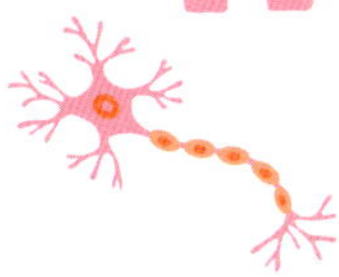

BY ALICE PEEL

ILLUSTRATIONS BY BECK FEINER

NEWSOUTH

CONTENTS

INTRODUCTION

THERE IS SOMETHING YOU NEED TO KNOW

Is the daddy-long-legs the most venomous spider in the world?

Where in the world do people live the longest?

How do you go about being a 'good enough' kid?

Why does losing feel like rubbish and what can you do about it?

This guidebook will answer all these questions and MORE. This book is for you, kid. Yes, your parents or teacher picked it out for you. Maybe they forced it down your throat or left it somewhere obvious and you stumbled upon it and picked it up. But hey, it's in your hands now, so why not read it? Do it for the trees! They worked hard to give you these pages. Nah, actually, do it for yourself!

BUT WHY SHOULD I READ IT? ~~GREAT, AWESOME,~~ GOOD ENOUGH QUESTION, KID!

Because life can be hard. And sometimes we forget this and freak out if we fight with friends or when we don't win or if we do a handstand with a dress on. Awkward. But here's the thing. We *can* do hard things. Especially if we have good people around us and if we know what our options are. Those options lie here, within the pages of this book. You will learn about the brain. You will practise skills to build resilience. And you'll hear from some real-deal kids who faced tough times and used strategies (that you can try as well) to get through them. The main thing you'll learn (spoiler alert) is ...

you already ARE a good enough kid!

WHO IS THIS BOOK FOR?

If you have a heart that is beating, then this book is for you.

HOW DO I READ THIS BOOK?

It will make more sense if you start from the beginning and read the chapters in order. Each chapter poses a question, so if you need the answer *now*, skip ahead. This book is meant to be graffitied in (unless you've borrowed it from a library)! I'm not talking about the tags you see down at the skate park, but your own, unique and original ideas, artworks and musings. We have created signposts throughout each chapter so you and your parents, carers or teachers can see what's coming. Sometimes the same signpost will be repeated. Look out for these symbols:

LISTEN UP, LEGENDS if you are daydreaming, it is time to quit it and listen. I mean it. Focus, people.

TAKE IT OR LEAVE IT as the title suggests, these are recommendations for things you can try. You can choose to accept or ignore these!

THE ANIMAL HELPER each chapter will have a key part of the brain represented by an animal: your 'helper'. Think of the animal as a guide; they assist you with learning the content and applying it to your life.

BREAK IT DOWN, NOW this is where I delve deeper into the topic, break down some of the tricky concepts and reflect on what it means. As you come to read this section, I suggest singing out: 'Break it down, now'! Simply for the sheer joy of it.

BRAIN BREAK gosh, you will need one by now! You will find answers at the back of the book.

ORDINARY MAGIC your chance to hear from an actual kid about the topic.

DETECTIVE TIME no crimes to solve, I'm sorry, but it is your chance to conduct your own mini research project.

PRACTICE MAKES PROGRESS as the title suggests, this is your time to practise some of the ideas that have been thrown your way.

WHO IS ANSWERING THE QUESTIONS?

Me! Alice. I'm a primary school teacher, writer, mother of goats, dogs and small humans. I live on Dharawal Country in a beautiful town called Jamberoo. I work for an incredible social venture called Grow Your Mind with one of my best friends, Tina. She's a legend, a health professional, lover of the ocean, dancer and Mumma to two awesome and totally good enough kids. She lives on Bidjigal, Birrabirragal and Gadigal Land in gorgeous Bronte.

Tina and I spend our days hoping to inspire you, your parents and your teachers to take care of your mental health*. We all have it, and we can all learn to look after it. We created a mental health podcast for children that has been listened to in over 140 countries. We teach kids about their brain, emotions, character strengths and how to make (and keep) fantastic friends. We want you, dear reader, and all kids out there to have a toolbelt of wellbeing strategies. You can use these tools to become resilient and flourish throughout your life. Reading this book will help you feel less stuck or scared by uncomfortable feelings. You'll be inspired to move your body, show kindness and notice the good.

*MENTAL HEALTH

Everyone thinks 'mental health' is about being unwell. But it's actually about so much more. When we talk about physical health, we talk about more than heart attacks, knee reconstructions or asthma. We talk about how fit you are, your ability to move and your strength. Same goes for your mental health – we talk about your ability to cope, to function, to make decisions, to build positive relationships and more. Plus, we are all on a mental health continuum, which means our mental health can sit anywhere between well and unwell (see Fancy Exhibit A). It is normal to move up and down this continuum throughout our lives.

FANCY EXHIBIT A – MENTAL HEALTH CONTINUUM

In case you're still unconvinced, the University of Wollongong studied Grow Your Mind and found our way of doing things really works! So, essentially, you can believe 99% of the things we say. The missing 1% is because Tina claims she has the best dog in the world when, clearly, *I* do. That's okay, I give her permission to be human and make mistakes.

This book is about helping you get mentally fit, which takes practice. You will hear me bang on about *practice makes progress* a million and one times. Because just like you can't go for one run and announce you are 'fit for life', you can't read the things in this book and claim to be mentally fit FOREVER. You need to practise. At the end of each chapter there's a dedicated section for the mental fitness* skills you need to practise for the **rest of your life.** Wait! Don't run away! If you start practising now, it will become a habit and the whole 'rest of your life' thing will be totally doable.

*MENTAL FITNESS

Just as you build physical fitness by moving your body, you can build 'mental fitness' by consistently and intentionally doing things that take care of your mental health. When we are mentally fit, we feel like we can deal with whatever the day throws at us.

I know you're pumped to get mentally fit, but before you jump into Chapter 1, there is something you need to know

YOU HAVE ANIMALS INSIDE YOUR BRAIN!

You read that right! There are animals inside your brain. Well, technically there aren't *real* animals living inside your brain. That would be stinky and loud. But knowing a bit about how our brain works and what keeps it running can really help you out.

Tina and I have come up with animals which represent key parts of your brain. There are big words to describe the brain bits; words like 'prefrontal cortex', 'amygdala' and 'hippocampus'. We *could* use these words, but we've done some research on memory and here's the thing – you're much more likely to remember a Wise Owl who makes good decisions rather than the prefrontal cortex. It's easier to picture a Guard Dog barking loudly to protect you, rather than trying to recall the squishy blob known as the amygdala. We'll remind you of the animal and their fancy brain name throughout the book.

ANIMAL AND BRAIN FACTS

Before we wow you with neuroscience and animal facts there's one thing to remember: the best thing about science is that it's progressive. This means we learn more as research and technology improve. Sometimes we realise we've been mistaken. This is not about saying – gotcha! Instead, it's about always being open to learning and rethinking. So go forth, share these facts AND be open to some of them changing in the future.

ANIMAL FACTS: DOGS

Did you know that a dog's sense of smell is over 100,000 times more sensitive than a human's? This means they can smell things we can't - things like BOMBS and even DISEASES in the human body!

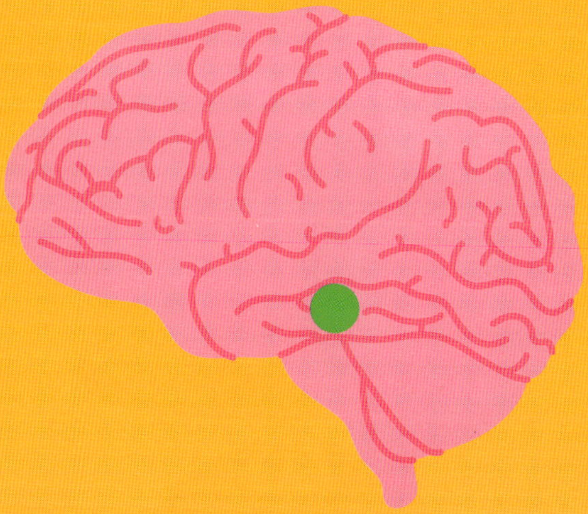

BRAIN FACTS: THE AMYGDALA AKA THE GUARD DOG

Have you ever heard of a sentinel? It's basically a guard – a person that keeps watch. It could be a soldier, or it could be a GUARD DOG! That's why I want you to imagine having a Guard Dog in your brain. It's on alert, growling and barking when something important is happening.

The Guard Dog (your amygdala) is there to protect you. But sometimes it treats losing at handball as a high-level security breach. Mistakes like missing a shot or making a spelling error can prompt the same reaction from your Guard Dog as breaking both legs or being chased by a hungry crocodile.

The amygdala has a bad reputation for creating emotional outbursts or making you lose your cool, but it also helps us feel joy or work out if something is a threat, a challenge or an opportunity.

ANIMAL FACTS: OWLS

Did you know that owls are excellent predators? They have been known to grab ducks out of the water, swoop down on squirrels, snatch snakes, dig out hidden mice under the snow and nab bats from the evening air.

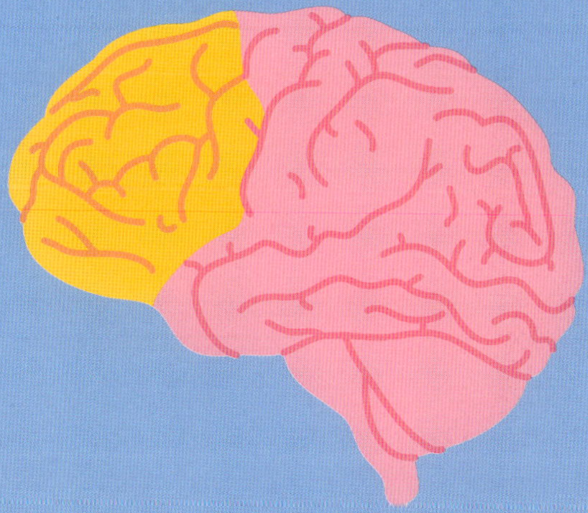

BRAIN FACTS: PREFRONTAL CORTEX AKA THE WISE OWL

The prefrontal cortex lies at the front of our brains. It helps us work out if something is good, bad, better, same or different. It predicts what might happen if we do certain things. That's why we call this region of the brain 'the Wise Owl', because we like to imagine a large, majestic bird deciding the best course of action. The Wise Owl is the king of self-control. It will not steal a chip from your hands. It is waiting, watching, deciding and pouncing. That's why this part of the brain is NOT called the Wise Seagull!

ANIMAL FACTS: ELEPHANTS

Did you know that when elephants swim they use their trunk as a snorkel? They also spend between 12 and 18 hours eating every day and you know what that means? Each elephant creates about ONE TONNE of poo every week! That's equivalent to two grand pianos or a VW Beetle in POOP.

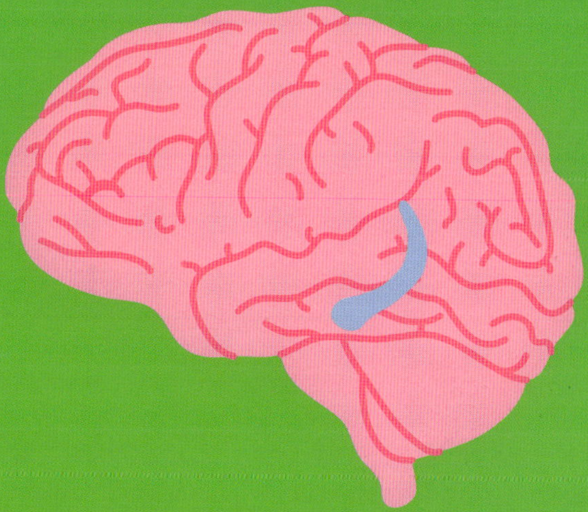

BRAIN FACTS: HIPPOCAMPUS AKA THE ELEPHANT WHO TRIES TO REMEMBER

The hippocampus lies deep inside the brain. Its name comes from the Greek words *hippo*, meaning 'horse', and *kampo*, meaning 'sea monster', as its shape resembles a seahorse. It helps turn short-term memory into long-term memory. We call this part of the brain the 'Elephant who tries to remember' because elephants actually have a brilliant memory. They can remember where water sources are located and lead their herd to them. Researchers even found that if a human hurts an elephant, they will hold a grudge against that person!

ANIMAL FACTS: OCTOPUSES

Did you know that octopuses are masters of a costume change? They can change the colour, pattern and texture of their skin within a fraction of a second. They have even been known to use items in their environment such as shells as camouflage.

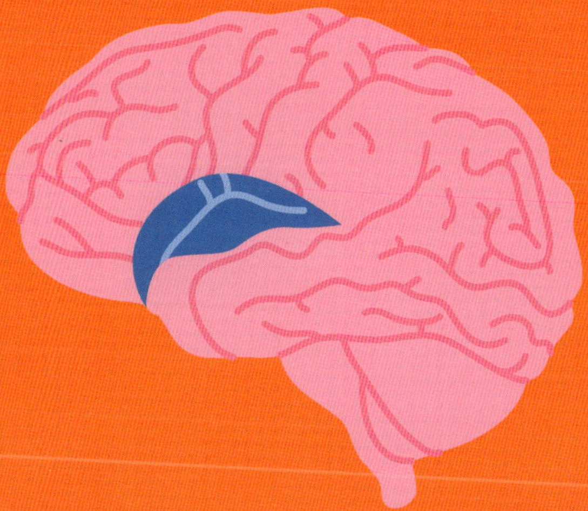

BRAIN FACTS: INSULAR CORTEX AKA THE SENSITIVE OCTOPUS

Neuroscientists believe this part of our brain is crucial to understanding what it feels like to be human. The insular cortex reads our body, noticing physical sensations such as our heart racing, a queasy stomach or sweaty palms. It then creates feelings that can bring about actions. We call it 'the Sensitive Octopus' because an octopus reacts to feelings of fear by dramatically changing colour, shape and size! Did you know that an octopus's arms are lined with suckers that include cells for neural processing of touch and taste signals? It would be like us using our fingers to touch and taste something at the same time! Our insular cortex (firmly lodged in our head) reads that we are hungry, so we start to eat. It also reads other people's emotional states and situations and helps us to behave with empathy and compassion.

ANIMAL FACTS: SOOTY SHEARWATER

Did you know that the Sooty Shearwater travels 500 kilometres a day for a whole year? It has the most persistent focus in the animal kingdom. If it loses focus, it won't reach its migration goal.

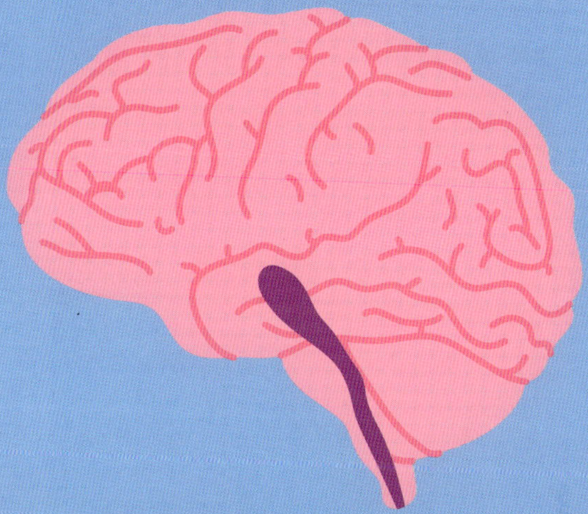

BRAIN FACTS: RETICULAR ACTIVATING SYSTEM AKA THE SIFTING SOOTY

The reticular activating system can be found in the brain stem. It's an intricate network of nerve pathways which connects the brainstem to the prefrontal cortex. One of its jobs is to filter out unnecessary information. We called our reticular activating system 'the Sifting Sooty' because we were inspired by a bird called the Sooty Shearwater, which can travel incredible distances in a day, taking a ridiculous amount of focus. It can't get distracted by other good-looking birds or the sweet smells of human food or gorgeous rainbows. It needs to fly or die. We like to imagine you daydreaming in class when your Sifting Sooty whispers in your ear – 'Listen up!' – and you snap back to attention!

SEE, THERE ARE ANIMALS IN YOUR BRAIN!

CAN YOU LOCATE THEM BELOW?

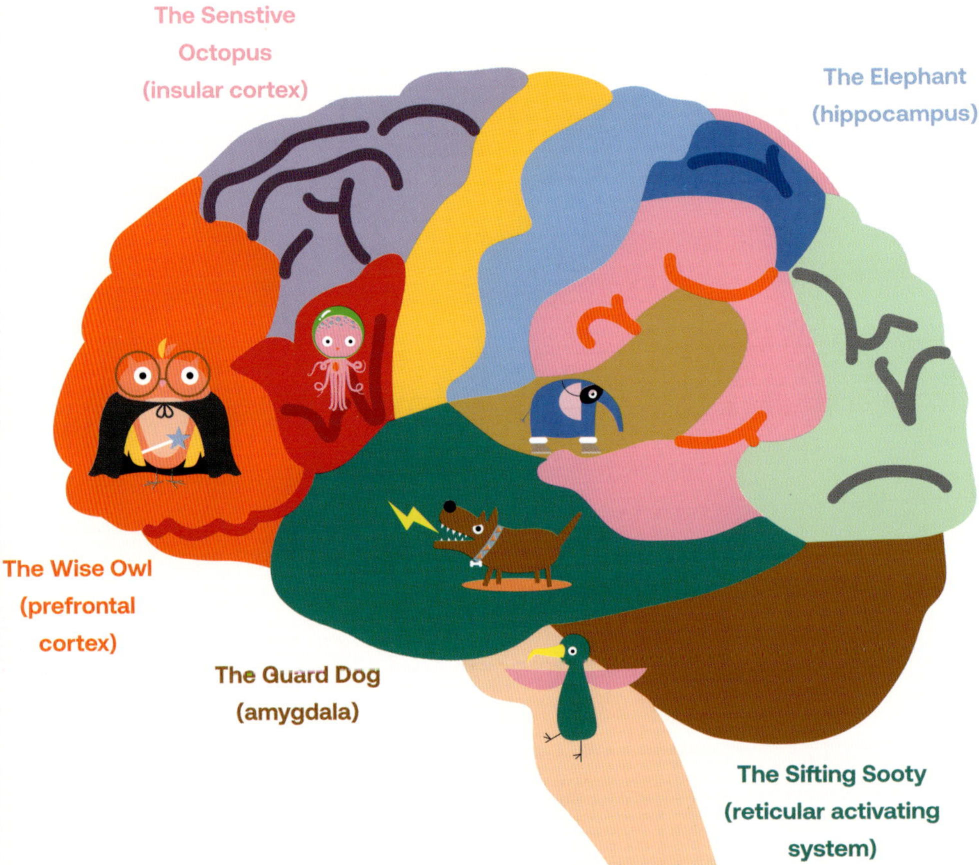

HOW WILL THE ANIMALS HELP YOU BE A GOOD ENOUGH KID?

They won't. Remember: you already ARE a good enough kid. 'Brilliant,' you say, 'I don't have to read this guidebook'. Well, maybe you don't. But honestly, between you and the pages of this book, do you really celebrate and feel good enough *always*? There is a book by Charlie Mackesy called *The Boy, The Mole, The Fox and the Horse*. In the story, the fox tells the boy:

You know sometimes your mind plays tricks on you. It can tell you you're no good, that it's all hopeless. But I've discovered this. You are loved and important and bring to this world things no one else can.

This book is about challenging some of those 'tricks' the mind can play on you. For example, do you have moments where you wish you were *better* or *different*? Have you been in situations where you don't know how to solve a problem? Or perhaps you struggle to cool your jets when things don't go exactly as you planned? Maybe you feel rubbish because you never win? Or perhaps you're rubbish at being the winner? You might struggle to share your friends. Or maybe you can't get off your device and while you love it, you kind of know you should shower from time to time? This book will give you the tools to navigate these issues.

Each animal will guide you through the chapters, helping you celebrate your good enough ways and inspiring you to be the kinder, more helpful version of yourself. And sometimes, as Yoda said, 'You must unlearn what you have learned'. Before picking up this book, you may have believed that mistakes were to be avoided or that a fight with a friend means it's time to change your name and move to Costa Rica. This book may challenge your beliefs. So, when it comes to any suggestion I put forward, you can take it or leave it. Just go forth with an open mind.

MAY THE FORCE BE WITH YOU.

CHAPTER 1:
HOW TO GET OUT OF A TRAP

(READ THIS OUT LOUD USING YOUR BEST ANIMAL VOICES)

IF YOU HAD SPRINKLES, THEN YOUR ICE CREAM WOULD BE BETTER
IT'S A TRAP
BUT MY ICE CREAM *WOULD* BE BETTER WITH SPRINKLES
IMAGINE YOU HAVE A SPRINKLED ICE CREAM, BUT YOUR MATE HAS A FLAKE
NOOOOOOO
SEE, IT'S A TRAP, YOU GET WHAT YOU WANT BUT YOU ALWAYS WANT MORE
HOW DO I GET OUT OF IT?
FOCUS ON WHAT YOU DO HAVE INSTEAD OF WHAT YOU DON'T
THE GRASS ALWAYS LOOKS GREENER ON THE OTHER SIDE
ANOTHER SAYING?
YEAH, BUT DO YOU THINK IT'S TRUE?
THAT THE GRASS IS GREENER OR LOOKS GREENER?
BOTH
MAYBE THE GRASS IS GREENER WHERE YOU WATER IT?

HOW TO GET OUT OF A TRAP

Picture this. Your name is Bear Grylls. You are the host of a show called *Man vs. Wild*. In each episode you are stranded in the wild and need to find a way back to civilisation. Sometimes you must make tricky choices to survive, such as drinking your own urine or eating the eyeballs off a sheep. Other times you might find yourself trapped. Maybe you've jammed your body in a dark, narrow cave. You need to get unstuck before hypothermia sets in and the flood waters rise. How do you get yourself out of this trap?

WELL. UMMM. AHHH. HONESTLY ... I HAVE NO IDEA! SORRY!

This chapter isn't about surviving physical traps in the wild. It's about overcoming mental traps. And there are many. The trap I'm referring to is called the 'If and Then' trap. It's when you believe that *if* you had certain things, or were different in some way, *then* you would feel better. The seagull from the comic was not just trapped physically, it was caught up in the fear of missing out and couldn't delight in what it already had. This chapter is about how to get unstuck from the 'If and Then' trap. For real, I promise! I actually *do* know how to get out of this kind of trap. I'll also show you a couple of tricks to avoid falling into the 'If and Then' trap in the first place, so you can continue in your quest to be a ~~sensational~~, ~~fantastic~~, good enough kid.

SIFTING SOOTY

WHAT'S THAT? YOU NEVER FALL INTO THE 'IF AND THEN' TRAP?

I'm sure you're an honest person ... but let's just check that statement. Have you ever wished you owned something and you were 1000% sure that **IF** you had it **THEN** you would be cooler, happier, smarter, quicker or better? Here's the thing. Our brains fall into this 'If and Then' trap a lot ...

'If my ice cream had two scoops instead of one, then I would be happier.'

'If I played touch footy as well as Fatima, then I'd be more popular.'

'If I get an A in my test, then my parents will be proud of me.'

IT'S A MIND TRAP

When you live by the 'If and Then' belief system, feeling content or joyful is always something that *might* happen in the future. It means your happiness is always just out of reach; it's *conditional* and depends on external things. For example, you might spend a lot of time believing that being different from who you are will make you happy. While having dreams and goals are fantastic, you may never actually get the dream thing. You may never have long legs, olive skin or the ability to kick like Sam Kerr. And if you *do* get the 'If' thing, it might not have as big an impact on your life as you expected. And then you find yourself wanting something different.

The 'If and Then' trap leads to other mind traps too. Just like when your leg gets stuck in quicksand, it sucks in your hip, your torso and your arms. Traps can lead to other traps. Still not convinced it's a big problem?

FOUR MORE BIG PROBLEMS WITH THE 'IF AND THEN' TRAP

Problem 1: You fail to notice and appreciate all that you are and already have.

Problem 2: It leads to comparison; you focus on what other people have and can do. This is a slippery slope to jealousy.

Problem 3: As soon as you get the thing you really wanted, you start looking for something else.

Problem 4: You miss the main event – again and again – until you take your last breath. What's the main event? Great question. The main event is NOW.

There are two ways to get out of the 'If and Then' trap ...

SOLUTION NUMERO #1 ... CALL ON YOUR SIFTING SOOTY

Just like our ice cream-obsessed seagull friend at the beginning of the chapter, we need our Sifting Sooty to help us focus on what's REALLY important. All day long you are being bombarded by sounds, smells and sights. The Sifting Sooty is the part of your brain that filters out unnecessary information, so the important stuff gets through. The Sifting Sooty will help you focus on all that you are and all that you have. But how will the Sifting Sooty help you out of this mind trap? You may be fantastic at soccer and drawing, but all you can focus on is your inability to swim super-fast or be in the top maths group. The key word here is *focus*. We can train our brains – our Sifting Sooty – to shift the focus from what we *don't* have, to what we *do* have. If we don't train our brains to do this, we can find ourselves being engulfed by the green-eyed monster* aka problem #2 – jealousy.

*Pssst – the green-eyed monster is a metaphor. William Shakespeare used it to describe jealousy in his play, *Othello*. In this cautionary tale, Othello murders his kind wife based on misinformation and extreme jealousy. The green-eyed monster can destroy people if it's left unchecked. It must be tamed with generous assumptions and self-control.

Jealousy, envy and comparison are all BFFs. Comparison means we notice the similarities or differences between two things or people. Jealousy and envy* are the feelings you have when you don't just notice the differences, you feel afraid, frustrated and angered by them.

*JEALOUSY VS. ENVY

ENVY – we want something that someone else has.

JEALOUSY – we fear changes in a relationship or losing a relationship altogether. For example, you have a best friend. A new kid arrives at school and becomes their friend too. You are worried that the relationship will change.

FOR THE SAKE of simplicity and because 99.95% of our population also get envy and jealousy a little muddled, we will predominantly be using the term 'jealous' in this good enough book.

COMPARISON EXAMPLE:

You have longer legs than me and lots of friends.

ENVY

I wish I had lovely long legs like yours.

JEALOUSY

Show off. My best friend wants to play with you more than me because of your long legs.

Here's the thing. Comparison can have a knock-on effect; it can become envy or jealousy. In fact, I hereby call comparison the joy thief. Well, it may have been called that already by US President Theodore Roosevelt in 1909, but I'm laying claim to it now.

What on earth does that mean? How could comparison be the thief of joy? If our Sifting Sooty is untrained, we might focus on all the better things someone else has or does, rather than focusing on the things we already have. That makes comparison a thief; it steals the joy we have right now.

We can **train** our Sifting Sooty to solve this problem by noticing when we are comparing ourselves with others, and actively thinking about the things we DO have. Because we all feel jealous and we all compare. This is normal and part of being a human being – or a snail (actually, we're still waiting for confirmation about the snail fact)!

Here's an example of training your Sifting Sooty to notice when you're comparing It can help you get out of the trap by *looking* for what you *do* have:

WHAT IS WRONG WITH JEALOUSY AND ENVY?

Ah, did you not read about Othello?! I admit, that's quite an extreme example. Relax, just because you feel jealous does not mean you're on the path to destroying others. In fact, there is NOTHING wrong with jealousy or envy. They're normal emotions. But the problem is we don't often *own* that we feel jealous or envious. Instead, we hide it and find ways to bring the other person down. We might spread rumours about them or say little put-downs to boost our own confidence.

The thing is, when you act on jealousy, the person who will be left with the least amount of self-worth (good feelings about yourself) will be YOU. And it's all because you're stuck in a scarcity* mindset.

***Scarcity**

The state of being in short supply. For example, there's a scarcity of water in the desert.

Scarcity happens. We run out of water while hiking. Floods ruin crops and create a scarcity of, say, bananas. But there's not a scarcity of talents, strengths and opportunities to succeed in life. And when you get stuck in jealousy for too long, you have this unhelpful mindset which tells you that you'll never do well because someone else has won. Your Sifting Sooty can help get you out of this trap. Ask yourself:

WHAT AM I FOCUSING ON?

IS IT HELPFUL TO FOCUS ON THIS?

WHAT WOULD HELP ME FOCUS ON THE THINGS I ALREADY HAVE RIGHT NOW?

And the answer to that final question lies in solution #2.

SOLUTION NUMERO #2: GRATITUDE

Gratitude will help overcome all four of the problems created by the 'If and Then' trap. And yes, I can see your eyes rolling at the mention of gratitude. I hear you moan and complain. To be fair, gratitude has a bad reputation and, if it's misused, it can make you MORE unhappy and further stuck in your mind traps. Here are some examples of misuse:

HEY, YOU OKAY?

YEAH, JUST SCRAPED MY KNEE, IT REALLY HURTS.

WELL, SOME PEOPLE DON'T HAVE KNEES, SO HOW ABOUT YOU FEEL THANKFUL FOR YOUR SCRAPED KNEE?

OKAY ...

MUM, NONE OF THE KIDS LET ME SIT WITH THEM AT LUNCH TODAY.

DID YOU GET TO EAT LUNCH?

YEAH ...

FOCUS ON THAT. THERE ARE KIDS STARVING IN AFRICA.

This kind of 'gratitude' is why we may fantasise about flipping the bird to an adult who tells us to be thankful, even when we're in distress. This type of gratitude is called 'toxic positivity'*.

***Toxic positivity:**

Toxic – poisonous, harmful, unpleasant, destructive
Positivity – the practice of being, or tendency to be, positive or optimistic in attitude
Toxic positivity – the pressure to stay upbeat no matter how bad one's circumstance is

And instead of feeling thankful, toxic positivity will make you feel alone and disconnected from the people around you. There are two important things to remember when it comes to gratitude ...

THING 1: GRATITUDE TAKES PRACTICE

Imagine you woke up one day and declared: **I am an Olympic pole vaulter**. Realistically, you'd need to practise first. Even real Olympic pole vaulters work their way up to throwing themselves over a 5-metre pole. They weren't just going about their daily chores of unloading the dishwasher or getting the milk before randomly finding a pole and using it to inject themselves into the sky. They practise, practise, practise. And remember – practice makes ~~perfect~~ progress. This book is about shaking off 'perfect' because there's no such thing. Getting better at something and trying hard is the key to feeling – and being – good enough. So, you have permission to grab a pen and put a line through *perfect* every time you see it written in this book. Go on – do it.

THING 2: IT'S ABOUT MAKING SPACE FOR THE GOOD

Gratitude is not something you have; it's something you do. And you do it to bring on the feeling of 'enoughness'. You **are** enough. You **have** enough.

You can acknowledge life's sadness and setbacks and make room for the good too. A bit like squeezing up on a sofa so your friend or dog can fit. The sofa still exists – you're still on it – you just made room for someone else. The thing with gratitude is that you need to actively look for the good because our brains won't do this by default.

So how does gratitude help you out of the 'If and Then' trap? You need your Sifting Sooty to help you scan for the good. Here are some ways you can practise it:

NON-PAINFUL IDEA #1

Draw your hand. In each finger write or draw something or someone that you are truly thankful for. Cool! Now each day look at your hand and say the things you are most thankful for.

CHALLENGE: If there is a person on your hand, go and tell them that you are grateful for them and explain why.

NON-PAINFUL IDEA #2

At the end of the day, even the worst day, ask yourself:
What were three good things that happened today?

PAINFUL-ISH IDEA #3

Write a letter or email to someone you truly appreciate and send it! Give lots of examples and make it super specific.

NON-PAINFUL IDEA #4

Mix up the way you practise gratitude, so you don't get bored. You could start a gratitude jar with your family. At dinner, everyone takes a moment to write or draw one thing they are thankful for. Each person could then share their thing and pop it in the jar. Or maybe the jar is full of 'good times', like an awesome surf or a funny moment when your whole family laughed. You could make Sunday dinners the time to randomly choose something to read out from the jar, or you could be ambitious and have it as part of every family meal.

You could 'pay it forward' – if someone is kind or helpful to you, make it your mission to be kind to someone else. Spreading kindness is a form of gratitude; you've noticed something good and now you intend to do good yourself!

BRAIN BREAK:

What animal am I?

I have three hearts, I can regrow lost arms and I've been around for about 296 million years. I can pull the arms off a crab and inject it with a paralysis venom which causes the crab's enzymes to dissolve its own muscles, then I suck the crab meat out like a milkshake.

(Check out the answers to Brain Break questions on pages 248–249.)

Share this fact with someone:

There is an animal called the Goliath tigerfish, which has shark-sized teeth and ambushes fish, crocodiles, humans and flying birds.

SHINE THE SPOTLIGHT ON ...

EDDIE JAKU

HOLOCAUST SURVIVOR + SPREADER OF LOVE

*"If you have the opportunity today, please go home and tell your mother how much you love her. Do this for your mother."**

**it could be your mother or someone else you love*

Research Challenge: find out more about Eddie. Why do you think we included his name and picture in a chapter about gratitude?

MAEVE'S STORY

Maeve loved all things science; it was how she and her best friend, Ava, had first bonded. They delighted in experiments together, such as Mentos in Coke, exploding volcanoes or trying to make water rockets launch. Maeve, however, always struggled with envy and jealousy. Ava seemed to have more of everything. She lived in a bigger house, she was smarter and better at music, art, sport – all of it.

Things came to a crunch when Ava became school captain. Envy engulfed Maeve. Instead of congratulating Ava, Maeve said she was a show-off and told others she boasted too much. Maeve tried to belittle her friend's success, but she only succeeded in making herself feel worse.

Maeve became a total grump at home. Eventually, her dad took her for a walk and got her to talk about what was going on. Maeve explained that she wasn't good at anything. There was nothing great in her life. Her dad listened carefully, then told her she would receive something the following day that would completely change her perspective.

Maeve could hardly sleep; she kept imagining the gift. Maybe it would be air pods or a new iPad or clothes? When her dad produced a gratitude journal the next day, Maeve was bitterly disappointed. He told her to write three things that went well and three things she was proud of about herself. Every. Single. Day. His parting words: 'Treat it like a science experiment. Just see what happens in three weeks if you do it'.

Maeve angrily scribbled:

What went well today? Dad left the room.
I am proud that I ... have a nose.

She read the first entry out loud to her dad. He just smiled and said, 'If you want to run an accurate experiment, you need to do it properly'.

Well, the three-week experiment turned into a year-long habit. Maeve started to appreciate the things she already had and the things she could do. She even found a way to make it up to Ava. She started to compliment her and finally apologised for being unkind.

Maeve still feels jealousy now, but it isn't the *only* thing she feels.

Listen to Grow Your Mind podcast episodes:
This Too Shall Pass
The Trap

Also, head to our Grow Your Mind website, click on the *How to be a Good Enough Kid* page and get a free copy of the activities.

And to practise some of the ideas from this chapter, check out the following two pages.

REFLECTIONS

Over the next week, I want you to grab a piece of paper and write down your reflections in response to these questions:

Monday
What were three great things that happened on the weekend?

Tuesday
Name two people you are thankful for. Why do you appreciate them?

Wednesday
Right now, what are you feeling thankful for? Why?

Thursday
When did you have a feel-good moment yesterday? When did you laugh?

Friday
Write a note to someone you feel thankful for and explain why, right now. Send/give it to them this weekend.

Saturday
One beautiful or interesting thing I saw today (can be small!)

Sunday
Today I am going to tell ______________ why I feel thankful to have them in my life.

THREE GOOD THINGS

Try thinking of three good things from each day. Switch on your Sifting Sooty before you begin. You can do this by naming one thing you can see, smell, hear, taste and touch. It's a little trick that helps you focus and be in the moment.

PRACTISE MIXING IT UP

Write down your answers to these questions on a piece of paper.

Monday: One act of kindness I can try today:

Tuesday: Three cool things that trees do are:

Wednesday: Google 'otters with their babies' (you are welcome).

Thursday: One thing I am really looking forward to:

Friday: Create a gratitude jar for your home, pop it on the kitchen table.

CHAPTER 2: HOW TO CALM YOUR FARM

(READ THIS OUT LOUD USING YOUR BEST ANIMAL VOICES)

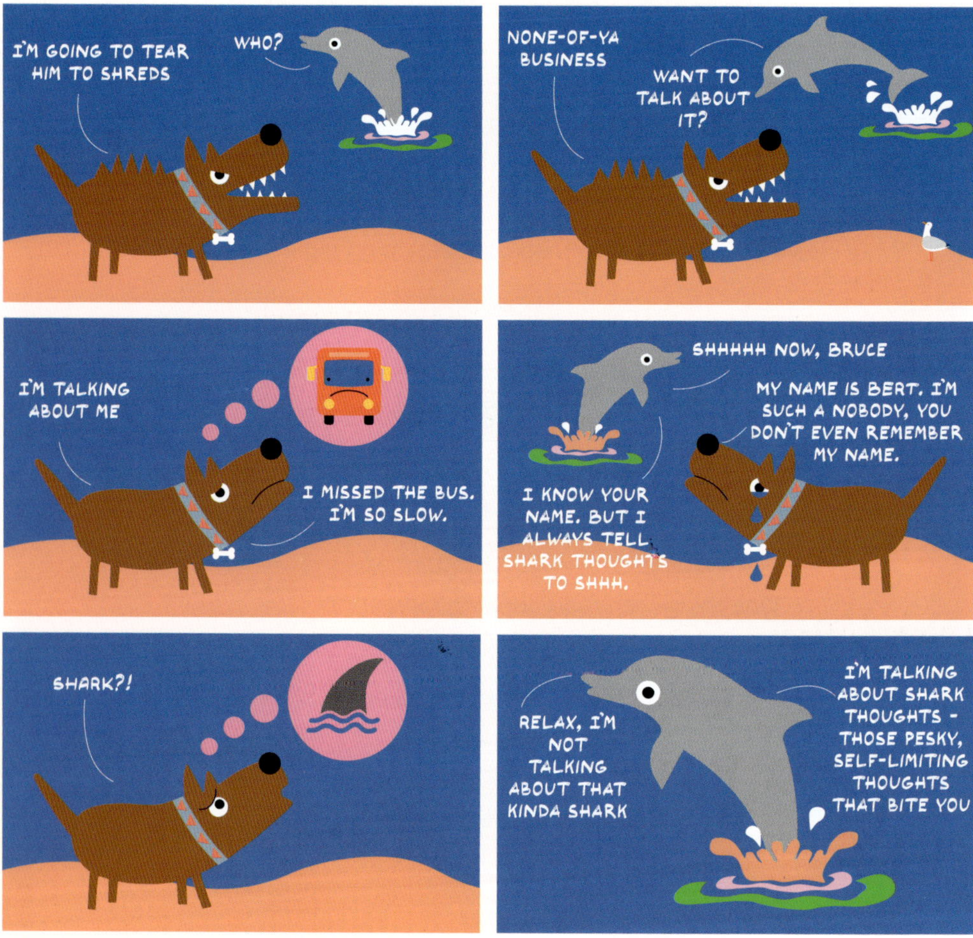

AND YOU CALL THAT BITING THOUGHT BRUCE?
YEAH, BUT YOU COULD CALL YOURS WHATEVER YOU LIKE
WHAT DOES A SHARK THOUGHT SOUND LIKE?
OH, YOU KNOW ... THINGS LIKE 'I'M SUCH AN IDIOT'
'I'M SO BAD AT DRAWING'
OK OK ... I GET IT
I'LL CALL MY SHARK THOUGHTS ALFRED, AFTER A BULLY I USED TO LIVE WITH
BOOM ... NOW JUST SAY IN YOUR HEAD, 'SHHH, ALFRED'
BETTER?
I'M STILL A LITTLE WORKED UP
YOU NEED TO COMPLETE YOUR STRESS RESPONSE CYCLE
WHAT THE?
CHILL, IT'S JUST DOING SOMETHING THAT HELPS YOU FEEL OK AFTER FEELING STRESSED
YOU COULD HOWL AT THE SKY, SPLASH YOUR FACE WITH WATER OR COME FOR A DIP WITH ME

HOW TO CALM YOUR FARM

Let's imagine it's Tuesday and you're at school. The only good thing about Tuesday is sport, which is coming up in the next 30 minutes. Suddenly, a teacher tells you it's cancelled. This is a blow. You're massively disappointed. You react as though your teacher just announced that break times are banned for life. In fact, fun is now a punishable crime. If he sees you enjoying yourself, you will receive detention for a year.

You yell. You complain. You cry about the injustices of the school system and kick your chair violently. It falls onto the floor and your poor-unsuspecting classmate trips over it and breaks her ankle in three places.

Yes, sport being cancelled is rubbish. Your reaction is a bit rubbish too. See, the problem isn't the anger you feel, it's the *behaviour* that comes with anger. You, me and the person next door are all capable of being the chair-thrower when we have **BIG** and **UNCOMFORTABLE** feelings. This is due to our cheeky, magnificent Guard Dog getting things a little wrong.

AREN'T GUARD DOGS THERE TO KEEP PEOPLE SAFE?

Have you ever walked to the shops to get milk because you're a saint disguised as a 12-year-old punk? There you are, giving up your free time, when you walk past some houses and suddenly a dog barks furiously at you. You're terrified. Luckily, there's a fence between you and those fangs.

The guard dog is doing its job: keeping her home safe. But you're not trying to steal her owner's Nintendo Switch. You're not breaking into a sweet old granny's house, wreaking havoc and whacking her on the head with a canvas bag (never plastic – see you really are a saint). And yet, the dog barks at you as if you were. Here's the thing, if the owner came out and told its guard dog that everyone was safe, or if the dog got to know you, it would eventually learn that you're not a threat. This is why our amygdala is such an important part of our brain, and why we call it the 'Guard Dog'. It's there, taking note of your surroundings, alerting you to important things. But it gets danger confused sometimes, a bit like how a smoke alarm, designed to warn you about fire, goes off when you burn the toast. With time, you can teach your brain to differentiate between real and perceived threats.

HOW IS THE AMYGDALA GOING TO CALM YOUR FARM?

We can help our Guard Dog and the Guard Dog can help us. There are loads of ways we can calm down when we feel big and uncomfortable feelings. Did you notice I didn't say *terrible* and *awful* feelings? That's because all feelings are welcome. All reactions are not. You can teach your Guard Dog by reminding it that **thoughts are not facts.** That way, it can challenge your really unhelpful thoughts. Let's call these thoughts 'shark thoughts', and not because there's anything wrong with real sharks. Sharks are an essential part of the ecosystem. The sharks in our heads, however, are unhelpful, harmful and untrue.

YOUR ANIMAL HELPER FOR THIS CHAPTER

I'm going to share five tried-and-tested ways to calm your farm. These five strategies are things you can do as you complete the stress response cycle*. They involve calming activities, just like the dolphin suggested in the opening story.

***Stress Response Cycle**

When we feel stressed, upset, scared, mad or frustrated by something, our body has a biological process with a beginning, a middle and an end. The beginning is when something happens inside or outside of our bodies that causes our Guard Dog to be alert. The middle is when our Guard Dog can really get barking. This can make it hard for the other animals to do their jobs. The end of the stress response cycle is when we choose an activity or strategy that helps us feel calm and safe again. Sometimes we forget to complete our stress response cycle.

NONE of these calming things will EVER work if you don't practise them. Remember: practice makes progress (never perfect). Also remember:

> 'Never in the history of calming down has anyone calmed down by being told to calm down.'
>
> **– Unknown**

THE STRESS RESPONSE CYCLE

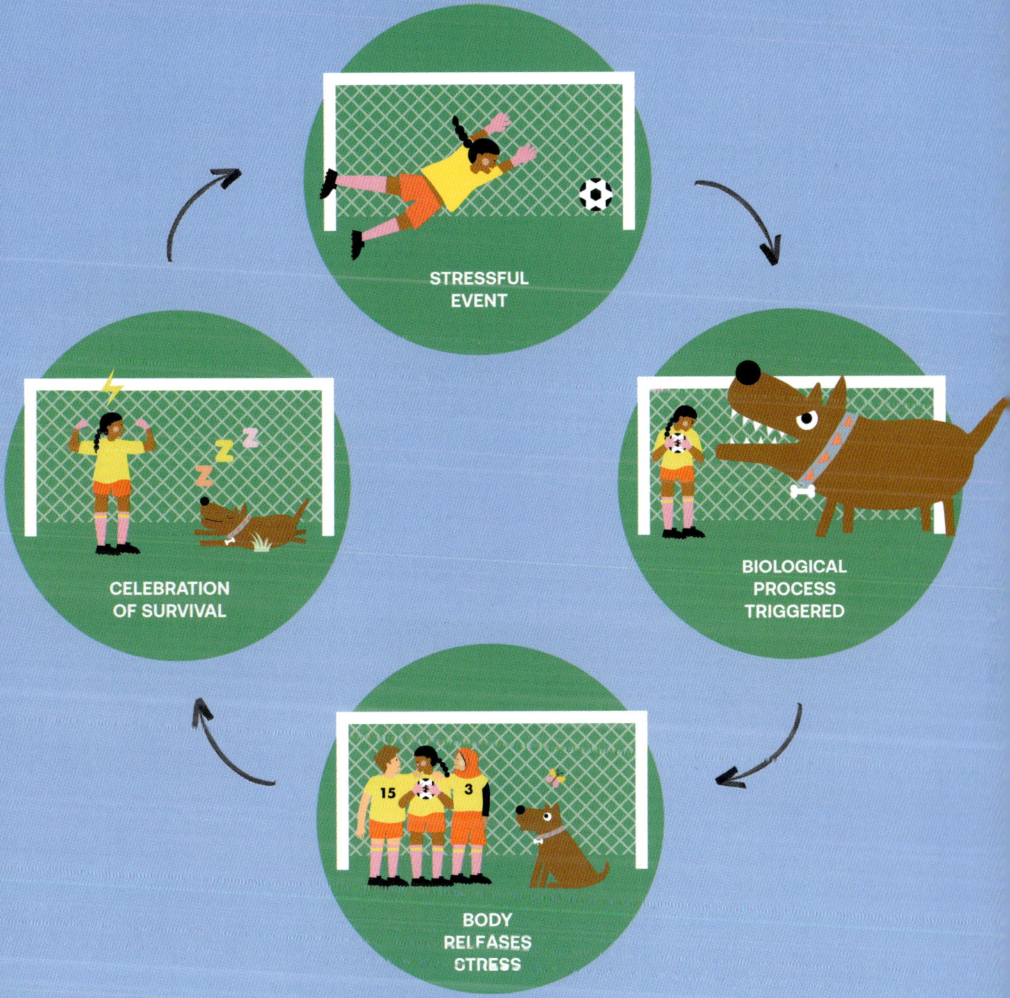

1
2
3
4
5

CALMING THING 1: BREATHE

You do it all the time. If you're not doing it, then you aren't reading or listening to this book. In fact, the game of life is up. So no, I'm not telling you to keep doing the regular breathing thing that keeps you alive. I'm talking about breathing slowly and mindfully*.

***Mindfulness**

Being in the present moment. You are aware of your surroundings. You do one thing at a time. You are not thinking about yesterday or tomorrow. You are here now. And when you start thinking about other things, you notice it, breathe and come back to what you are doing right now.

Use your Sifting Sooty to focus on your breath as you inhale and exhale. Breathe in slooowwwly, hold for two counts, then breathe out slooowwwly. Focus on your breathing. Don't worry if you're thinking about pizza. Just notice yourself inhaling and exhaling. Next, choose your own adventure and try one of these mindful breathing exercises.

BREATHING TECHNIQUES

Finger breathing
Hold your hand up. Using the index finger on your other hand, start tracing your thumb, sliding it upwards as you breathe in for three counts. When you reach the top of your thumb, slide it down the other side as you breathe out for three counts. Continue along each finger.

Anchor Breathing
Put your hand on your belly. Imagine a wild ocean. Imagine throwing an anchor into the ocean. Notice how you inhale and exhale and what your tummy does.

In for two out for four
Soften your eyes. Breathe in for two counts, hold your breath, then breathe out for four counts.

Square breathing
Grab a pencil and paper. You are going to draw a square. Breathe in as you draw one side. Hold your breath as you draw the next side. Breathe out for the next side. Hold your breath for the final side.

Breathing gives your Guard Dog a chance to work out whether there's danger. Think of it like a traffic light, telling a vehicle to stop before moving on. Let's say you notice yourself feeling angry. Before you react, you stop and breathe, giving your Guard Dog a moment to check with the other animals – am I scared but safe, or am I scared and in danger? What can I do? Who or what might help?

BREATHE
THINK
ACT

CALMING THING 2: WATER IS A GAME CHANGER

Okay, maybe you can't go for a swim or take a shower at school. Your art teacher is not going to appreciate you announcing you're off for a shower because you need to calm down. But at home you can! Even in winter, I promise you, you will never regret a swim. Cold water is a game changer for our mood. And recent research reveals the multiple mental and physical health benefits of cold water. But if you're short of an ice bath, don't underestimate the power of a bubbler. Splash your face with it. Just don't strip off and try to swim in it.

CALMING THING 3: NAME YOUR FEELINGS

No, I don't mean calling them Susie, Krishna or Shane. I'm talking about feeling jealous, frustrated, overwhelmed, peaceful, outraged, exhausted, disappointed, hurt, exasperated, excited, anxious, hopeful, calm and so on.

Dr Brené Brown is a social worker who's full of wisdom about feelings (among other things) and she's an incredible storyteller. She says: 'When we don't have the words for something, it doesn't exist'. Dr Brown goes on to explain that if you went to a doctor's appointment with a sore tummy, but you taped up your mouth and tied up your hands, it would be impossible for the doctor to understand you, and therefore impossible for them to help you.

It's the same issue with our feelings. We can't help ourselves if we can't identify what we're feeling. And our feelings are so often disguised as ANGER. You might actually be stressed, lonely, frustrated or disappointed, and yet you think you're feeling anger. You might get angry at someone else because your ice cream just melted or you didn't make the debating team, even though it's got nothing to do with them. Poor Nancy was just going about her day, collecting stamps, and she happened to smile at you. That's enough to unleash your Guard Dog with accusations like: 'Why are YOU laughing at me?'

When we name our feelings properly, we get to the source of the problem and tame our Guard Dog in the process. We 'name it to tame it'. I didn't come up with that catchy slogan. Dr Dan Siegel did. He's a psychiatrist, author and a world leader in something called 'neuroplasticity'*.

<u>*Neuroplasticity</u>

The capacity of the brain to change with learning and experience. Our brains are made up of billions of neurons, which send messages. When we learn something new, the brain makes stronger connections between neurons. This is why practice makes progress, because the neural connections get stronger. Our brains are not set in stone! They're always changing – this is what neuroplasticity is all about.

When we name our feelings and tame them, each and every time, our brain will eventually stop telling us to slam doors when we feel angry! What does 'name it to tame it' mean? It means that if you label your feelings accurately, you give the big and uncomfortable ones less power. Again, it's not about getting rid of these feelings – they are important. It's about having the power to choose what you do next, rather than letting your feelings push you to slam doors, shame others and resort to name-calling.

How many feelings do you think you could name right now? Brené Brown says we have 87. Yale University suggests there are 64 and they've even created a 'mood meter'. Either way, that's a lot of feelings to try and remember. We've included a sample here. Have you ever felt any of these feelings?

FURIOUS
SHOCKED
RESTLESS
NERVOUS
ANXIOUS

SURPRISED
JOYFUL
ECSTATIC
PROUD
UPBEAT

DISAPPOINTED
ASHAMED
LONELY
DISGUSTED
GLUM

THANKFUL
CALM
HUMBLE
BLESSED
FULFILLED

BRAIN BREAK:

What animal am I?

I have super skinny legs and people think I'm the most venomous spider. People also think I can't bite humans because my fangs are too small. The truth is, I *can* bite people, but I'm not deadly at all.

Share this fact with someone:

A green sea turtle can lay hundreds of eggs in one nesting season and, if they survive, those babies (known as hatchlings) will return to the same beach to lay their own eggs as adults.

CALMING THING 4: MOVE YOUR BODY

Skating, yoga, soccer, running, walking, skipping, swimming, handstands or jumping on the trampoline. JUST MOVE YOUR BODY! The Guard Dog relaxes when we move our body. It goes from hyper-alert and anxious to calm. This might be because movement floods us with endorphins*.

***Endorphins**

These are natural chemicals in the body that fight pain. Endorphins are released when a person gets hurt. They're also released during exercise or laughter. In addition to blocking pain, endorphins make you feel good.

When we move our bodies, we're not just helping our muscles, we're helping our mental wellbeing. When endorphins are released, we get a surge in energy levels, self-confidence and resilience.

CALMING THING 5: DO SOMETHING YOU LOVE

Paint, draw, cook, sing, imagine, daydream, journal, garden, dance or kick a ball! If you get absorbed by any of these things, you're helping your Guard Dog out of the threat response into a chilled state. If you can do an activity that's challenging, but not impossible, you may even find yourself in a flow state*. This can break a worry-cycle or shift a bad mood.

***Flow state**

A state of consciousness in which you perform and feel your best. Flow happens when you find something tricky, but not impossible. Losing yourself in flow activities has the capacity to improve your happiness.

If you're reading or listening to this, then you have a brain. And that brain loves to have adventures by imagining things. Worrying is one way your brain uses its imagination, but daydreaming is the flipside to worrying. And, when you imagine something wonderful, your brain lights up as if you're experiencing that wonderful thing. Try it now!

Imagine doing something you LOVE or being with someone who brings you joy. Close or soften your eyes and really imagine the feeling you have when you're doing this activity or being with this person.

You can use this strategy at school. It has a fancy name – 'breathing for coherence'. When you notice you're feeling overwhelmed, you can place a hand on your heart, close or soften your eyes and imagine someone you care about. You could also write a 'joy list', right now!

Here's one final suggestion for helping you calm your farm: think of where your problem might sit on a scale of problems. Now, this does NOT mean your problem means nothing. A problem can feel HUGE – that's okay. A feeling can feel HUGE too. Again, that's okay. The point of a problem scale is to check if your reaction matches the severity of the problem.

Imagine it's dinnertime. Your device has been taken from you because your family wants to connect. You react as though your mum just pooped on your food and your dad is forcing you to eat it. You scream and shout, but perhaps you just need to take a moment to ask yourself: how BIG is this problem? Is my reaction reasonable?

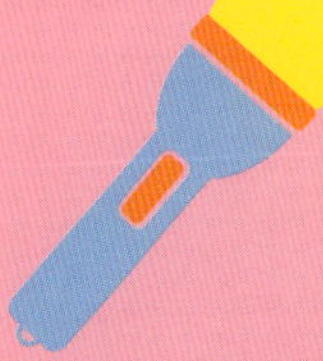

SHINE THE SPOTLIGHT ON ...

TURIA PITT

WRITER, ATHLETE, COACH, SPEAKER + SURVIVOR

"You've made it through another day. And then when a day was too hard, I'd break it up into hours, and I'd say you're still here, if another hour passed, you're still here."

Research Challenge: Turia Pitt is a bit of a legend. Find out why we included this image and quote from Turia in a chapter about ways to calm down.

TRAPPED IN A CAVE FOR TWO WEEKS

On 23 June 2018 in Chiang Rai, Thailand, a group of boys and their coach finished soccer training and decided to go for a little adventure. They went exploring in the nearby Tham Luang cave. They entered the dark cave, crawling through different passages, laughing and joking amongst themselves. They didn't realise it had started raining outside. Soon, water flooded the cave system. When they began walking back, they discovered a huge amount of water in their way. The cave was too narrow to swim through, and the next pocket of air was too far away The water was dark and muddy, making it impossible to see. They didn't have enough food or air in the cave. They were stuck. They were cold. They were afraid.

You'd think the boys would be distressed and anxious, but they were calm. How? The boys kept themselves busy, taking turns to try and dig their way out of the cave. Their coach, Eak, was a Buddhist monk before he became a football coach. Eak taught the boys meditation and breathing techniques to help them handle the stress. It kept them calm, ensuring they used as little air as possible.

On the ninth day, two torches appeared in the gloom. They were on the heads of two British divers, John Volanthen and Rick Stanton. The boys begged for food and the divers promised they would return with some – as well as a plan to get them out.

The boys were four kilometres from the cave mouth. The divers had gone through narrow, dark, muddy passages to get to them, which required a lot of skill. The whole world was watching the rescue team as they hatched a daring plan to retrieve the boys. By the time they launched the rescue mission, the boys had been trapped for over two weeks!

The plan was to attach each boy to a scuba diver, who would swim through four kilometres of pitch-black water until they arrived safely at the cave mouth. Can you imagine being hungry, tired and trapped for over two weeks and then having to swim that far? There was a high chance the boys would panic, which would not only risk their lives, but the lives of the rescuers as well. Enter Richard Harris, an Australian anaesthetist, and Craig Challen, a technical diver and cave explorer. Under their supervision, the boys were given anaesthetic before the journey, which needed to be topped up every 45 minutes. Together with an incredible team, Richard and Craig manoeuvred the boys out by holding onto their back or chest. In very narrow spots, they pushed the boys from behind. The divers navigated them through tight passages, careful to avoid dislodging their face masks against the craggy rock walls. At last, the boys and their coach were brought to safety.

So, short of taking anaesthetic when you feel worked up, nervous or frightened, why not try some mindful breathing?

Listen to Grow Your Mind podcast episodes: Power of the Pause (Song)

Can you memorise some of the lyrics? What is the message of the song?

Also, head to our Grow Your Mind website, click on the *How to be a Good Enough Kid* page and get a free copy of the activities.

And to practise some of the ideas from this chapter, check out the page opposite and the following two pages.

WEATHER REPORT

Sometimes it helps to distance yourself from big and uncomfortable feelings. Imagine they are clouds in the sky, passing by. You can describe them like a weather reporter:

Today, it's mostly cloudy with a chance of showers or heavy rainfall.

Answer these questions like a weather reporter:

WHAT DOES JOY FEEL LIKE IN YOUR BODY?

WHERE DO YOU FEEL FRUSTRATION IN YOUR BODY?

WHERE DO YOU FEEL ANGER IN YOUR BODY?

WHAT ARE SOME THINGS YOU CAN DO NEXT TIME YOUR INTERNAL WEATHER IS STORMY?

IT'S ALWAYS GOOD TO GET SOME POSITIVE EMOTIONS* IN YOUR LIFE TOO!

COMPLETE THIS TABLE AND USE IT WHEN YOU'RE STRUGGLING TO THINK OF WAYS TO COMPLETE A STRESS CYCLE.

* POSITIVE EMOTIONS HELP US FEEL GOOD. THEY PROMOTE WELLBEING AND RESILIENCE.

POSITIVE EMOTION	WHEN WAS THE LAST TIME I FELT THIS EMOTION?	WHEN DO I USUALLY FEEL THIS EMOTION?	WHAT CAN I DO TO CULTIVATE THIS FEELING?
Joy			
Gratitude			
Serenity			
Curiosity			
Hope			
Pride			
Playful			
Inspired			
Awe			
Love			

CHAPTER 3: HOW TO LIVE TO 100

(READ THIS OUT LOUD USING YOUR BEST ANIMAL VOICES)

I'M THINKING OF CHANGING MY COLOUR TO RED FOR THE NIGHT
WHAT'S THE POINT? YOU'RE GOING TO DIE ONE DAY.
I'D RATHER FOCUS ON HOW TO LIVE A LONG, HEALTHY LIFE
YES, THAT'S IT! THE ELIXIR OF LIFE. I SAW IT IN A MOVIE.
YOU DRINK IT AND BECOME IMMORTAL
OR JUST MOVE YOUR BODY, EAT HEALTHILY AND THEN YOU MIGHT LIVE A LONG LIFE
I THINK THE ELIXIR SOUNDS MORE APPEALING
SUIT YOURSELF
WHAT'S THAT?
A SEAWEED SMOOTHIE MY MUM MAKES ME DRINK
AN ELIXIR SMOOTHIE?
I'D RATHER BE MORTAL

HOW TO LIVE TO 100

What do most **centenarians** (a person who lives to be 100) have in common? Don't worry, they don't have to become a blob-like cyst like our friend, the immortal jellyfish, to reach their age.

I'm talking about super old people that are healthy in mind and body up until the end. What's their secret? Other than excellent genes ...

- They make movement a part of their day.
- They have a purpose. Maybe they volunteer, play a respected role in the community or help run meetings and events.
- They look after their family and their family look after them.

There is one more critical thing that people who live a long and healthy life share ...

Here's a clue: not having 'it' is more dangerous to your health than smoking 15 cigarettes a day. Not having 'it' can be more harmful to your health than obesity and not exercising. Is it an ice bath? No. Phew. According to an 85-year-old study, this critical thing is the secret to feeling content and living a longer life. 724 participants from all over the world were asked questions about their lives at 2-year intervals over the course of 85 years. And those that lived a happy and healthy life had one thing in common ...

HEALTHY RELATIONSHIPS!

And no, I don't mean your friends or family must be marathon-running, vegetable-eating legends. I'm talking about the relationship itself being healthy. You can be lonely because you live on a mountain with only miniature goats and flowers for company (my dream), or you can be lonely at school surrounded by 'friends' who make you feel like rubbish. Or perhaps you don't have any friends, but there are plenty of people in your class that you'd love to be friends with, you just don't know how to make that happen.

Having no mates at all, or mates where you can't be yourself, can have the same not-so-fantastic effects on your physical health. Healthy friendships, on the other hand, means you enjoy:

- lower rates of heart disease
- lower rates of dementia*
- less infectious illness because of a stronger immune system
- lower blood pressure

***Dementia**

The word 'dementia' describes a set of symptoms that can affect memory, problem-solving, language and behaviour over time. Someone with dementia may look healthy on the outside, but on the inside, their brain isn't working. They may struggle to remember who people are or the names of objects.

Now, I'm guessing that lowering your blood pressure or preventing dementia is low on your priority list, good enough kid. But I'm not asking you to eat your greens and drink water (even though I'd like you to). I want you to get some good friends in your life.

YOUR ANIMAL HELPER FOR THIS CHAPTER

SENSITIVE OCTOPUS

So, what is a healthy friendship?

Every friendship is different. But there are some golden guidelines for making and keeping a great friend, and for being a good human.

1

You don't have to be friends with everyone. But let's agree to be friendly to everyone.

2

Not all friends are good for us.

3

Conflict is part of every friendship. You don't need a BIG guard dog to deal with it.

4

Friendship is not like chocolate. It isn't meant to be perfect.

5

Generous assumptions help every friendship. What is the best you could assume about your friend?

6

Friendships change for lots of reasons (it still hurts though).

Let's take a quick look at each of these golden rules.

1. YOU DON'T HAVE TO BE FRIENDS WITH EVERYONE. BUT LET'S AGREE TO BE FRIENDLY TO EVERYONE.

Not everyone is for you, and you are not for everyone. It's okay if you're not friends with every single person in your class, sports team or band. But there's no reason, good enough kid, why you can't be friendly to everyone. This just means smiling, saying hi and waving. It's really not that hard.

2. NOT ALL FRIENDS ARE GOOD FOR US.

You might really like someone. You're desperate to be their friend but, for whatever reason, they don't bring out the best in you. Maybe you always feel slightly rubbish about yourself when you're around them. Perhaps you can't celebrate your wins because they get angry. Maybe they don't let you be friends with other people and threaten to stop talking to you if you make other friends. Listen to your Sensitive Octopus – do you get a queasy feeling in your tummy when you're with them? It's sometimes tricky to know which friends are good for us. Understanding what a healthy friendship looks like can help us work out when a friend is not good for us (more on that super soon).

3. CONFLICT IS A PART OF EVERY FRIENDSHIP. YOU DON'T NEED A BIG GUARD DOG TO DEAL WITH IT.

It's healthy and normal to disagree with your friends. It's not helpful if we unleash a big Guard Dog and yell, say unkind words or involve others unnecessarily.

4. FRIENDSHIP IS NOT LIKE CHOCOLATE. IT ISN'T MEANT TO BE PERFECT.

Friends will let us down. Friends tend to be humans and humans are not perfect. It's okay to be hurt, sad and disappointed when a friend does the wrong thing. But after a while you need to ask – *is it more important to hold onto my hurt or to hold onto this friendship?* Call on your Sensitive Octopus to imagine how it would feel if you did the wrong thing, and your friend wouldn't let it go.

5. GENEROUS ASSUMPTIONS HELP EVERY FRIENDSHIP. WHAT IS THE BEST YOU COULD ASSUME ABOUT YOUR FRIEND?

We have these incredible brains that make up stories all the time about everything. We get our feelings hurt. Perhaps you aren't invited to a sleepover, or your friend doesn't sit with you at lunch. You might send them a message and they don't reply. Our brains will create a story to make meaning of these things. And often that story in our head will have us assuming the worst, rather than the best. Our brains jump to conclusions such as: 'They don't like me anymore' or 'They're ignoring me because they're annoyed or bored with me.'

I'm not going to lie; it's hard to assume the best. Sometimes people can be cruel. They can say horrible things about your appearance or ask, 'What's that terrible smell?' every time you walk past them. Maybe they purposefully knock over your books and then smile. This is not the time for a generous assumption; instead, this is the time for stopping the unkind behaviour. However, there are 1001 other times in a day when we create stories about what people are doing or feeling that aren't helpful. This can cause unnecessary issues in a friendship. Try and ask yourself, what is the most generous assumption I could make about my friend? For example, 'They didn't speak to me because they're tired or busy ... they weren't setting out to hurt me.'

The Sensitive Octopus can help you with this. It can help you imagine what the other person might be thinking, going through or doing.

6. FRIENDSHIPS CHANGE FOR LOTS OF REASONS (IT STILL HURTS THOUGH).

Even when we make a truly brilliant friend, it's not a given that they'll always be our friend. Friendships take work. You will stuff up; your friends will too. Your interests will change, and theirs will too. This is normal. It doesn't stop it from hurting. So be kind to yourself.

BRAIN BREAK:

What living thing am I?

I'm so small you can only see me with the help of a microscope. I help you digest food and I tune up your immune system. There are millions of me in your body. I'm found in food too.

WHAT'S THE 'HEALTHY' PART OF A FRIENDSHIP?

Just as there are some key ingredients to make bread or a cake – flour, salt, water, eggs and sugar – there are also some key ingredients to maintaining a healthy friendship. So, what would be in a healthy friendship ingredient list? If I was baking, my recipe would include:

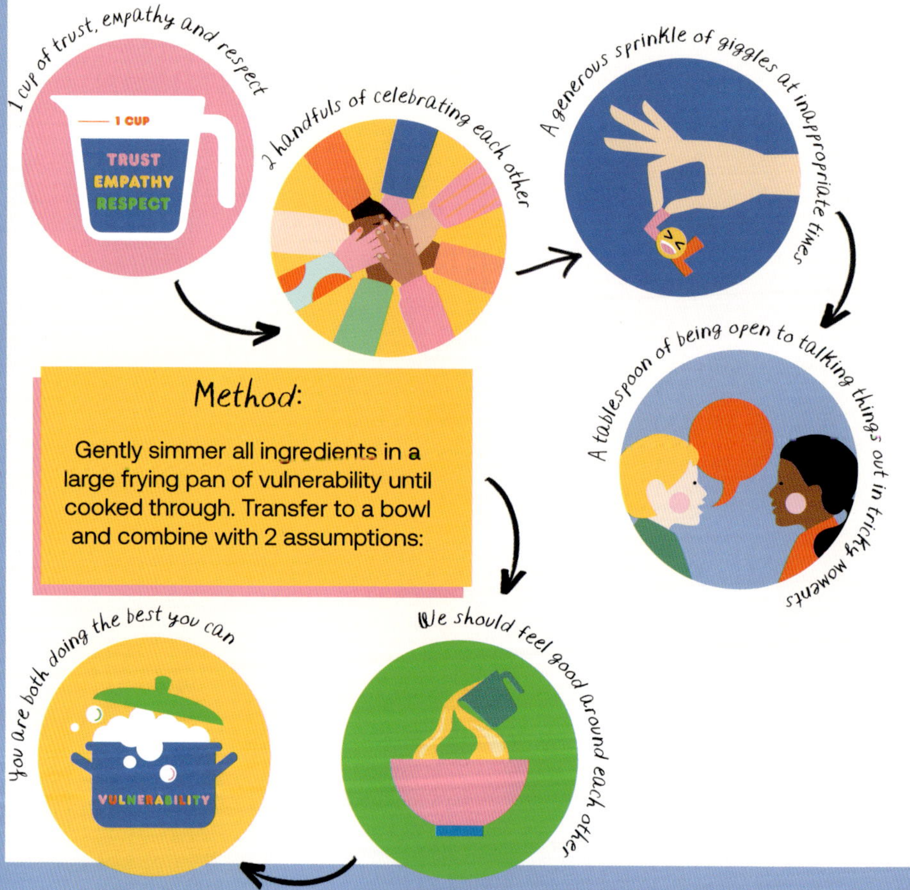

Method:

Gently simmer all ingredients in a large frying pan of vulnerability until cooked through. Transfer to a bowl and combine with 2 assumptions:

HOW DO YOU KNOW WHEN YOU'RE IN AN UNHEALTHY FRIENDSHIP?

- I often feel like I have done the wrong thing
- They laugh at me, not with me
- After being with them, I feel bad about myself
- I often feel let down
- I'm not sure how to act around them
- They don't like me spending time with other friends

If this sounds like how you feel with a friend, what can you do about it? You deserve to be treated with respect. It's okay to stop being friends with someone who makes you feel terrible. If you want to try and save the friendship, try these steps:

- Take three deep breaths
- Call on courage. Ask to talk to them about it alone.
- Use 'I' sentences and be specific. For example, 'I felt uncomfortable when ...'
- Talk about solutions and set your boundaries going forward
- Keep an eye out for signs that the friendship is getting unhealthy again. Be ready to follow through on your boundaries.

HOW DO I MAKE A FRIEND?

Now you know that friends will help you live to 105, how do you get one? There are five fairly bullet-proof (ish) ways to make a friend.

Smile and call someone by their name
Be yourself, everyone else is taken
Ask questions and listen
Join in
Your vibe attracts your people – be friendly

Let's jump into each of these. Even if you're a super-friendly, social human, sometimes making friends with people is tricky. They may feel they have enough friends or they might be shy.

SMILE AND CALL SOMEONE BY THEIR NAME

I know it might feel forced, but if you look miserable, then it's hard to make a connection. Go practise now. In the mirror. It will feel super weird. But remember, practice makes ... progress.

Now that you've become a smiling champion, it's time to remember their name. When you see them next, smile and say, 'Hi Shanushka' (or the name of the person you really want to be friends with). You don't need to get all strange and say Shanushka's name 100 times in a sentence: 'Really, Shanushka? That's amazing, Shanushka. Tell me more, Shanushka.' Trust me, it won't work. The real Shanushka found me a tad intense.

BE YOURSELF, EVERYONE ELSE IS TAKEN

Why? If you pretend you're super interested in basketball, Imagine Dragons or chess when you actually hate all of these things, it's going to be exhausting to keep it up. And people often see through a lie. So be you. If they don't like you, that's okay. There are more fish in the sea. And if they like you for who you are, life is going to be a lot more relaxing and fun. If you're a die-hard Dungeons & Dragons player, celebrate it. If you want to spend your days painting Warhammer figurines, tell people. If drawing comics sets your heart on fire, declare it. Be you.

ASK QUESTIONS AND LISTEN

It can be hard to ask questions. What questions should you ask? How do you ask them? Again, get your Sensitive Octopus to help you out here. How does it feel when people are friendly, show an interest in you and ask questions? Pretty good. So why not do the same for others? Just make sure that when you ask a question, you actually listen to the answer and aren't looking over their shoulder or down at your phone. A rockstar connection is when someone tells you their answer and you have a 'tell me more' vibe happening. For example:

YOU: HOW WAS YOUR WEEKEND?

**THEM: MY WEEKEND WAS GREAT, THANKS.
I WENT TO THE WATER PARK.**

**YOU: I LOVE WATER PARKS!
WHAT SLIDES DID YOU GO ON?**

A non-rockstar response would be silence. Or jumping in to tell them about how much you love cellos, ice cream or cats. Not relevant right now.

ASK TO JOIN IN

If the kids you'd like to be friends with are playing handball, basketball, robotics or survival tag, be brave and ask: 'Can I join in?' They may say 'no'. In which case, find out where they live and let me know. I jest!

A 'no' will hurt, but at least you know that these people may not *be* your people at this moment in time. *Hakuna Matata*. Look around, who else could you ask to join in with? You might realise there are no people at your school who will ever be *your* people. Luckily, you're a problem solver. You think to yourself: where else can someone find mates? You join a local sporting club, a band, scouts, an art class outside of school, a circus or chess club. There are an estimated two billion children in the world under 14. There will be other friends out there for you.

YOUR VIBE ATTRACTS YOUR PEOPLE

If you complain a lot or talk badly about others and create drama quickly, then these are the friends you will attract.

If you want loyal, kind, funny, genuine friends – be that person. Be friendly, even if you're shy. That's your vibe. Now go get your people.

SHINE THE SPOTLIGHT ON ...

OWEN AND MZEE:
AN UNLIKELY, LIFESAVING FRIENDSHIP

I can't speak hippo or tortoise, but I reckon Mzee, the old lonely tortoise might've said:

"Everyone thinks I saved Owen's life but, in fact, he saved mine."

Research Challenge: Look up the story of Owen and Mzee. Why do you think we have spotlighted them in this chapter about friendship?

UNHEALTHY FRIENDSHIP – INDIA FINDS HER VOICE

India was a kindergarten student when she noticed a new girl, Mary, sitting alone. India offered to play together and the two connected. A friendship started and playtime at school became more joyful. They had playdates at each other's houses. But in Year 1, things started to change. India felt like she was not allowed to play with anyone other than Mary. In fact, if India did play with someone different, Mary would sulk and threaten to no longer be her friend. This went on for AGES. The thing was, India was shy and lacked confidence. She felt confused by her friend's anger and possessive ways. She didn't want to go to school, but she couldn't explain why.

India knew that Mary struggled and was often sad. She didn't want to make things worse. But inside, India felt lonely. She longed to play with other kids and to choose how she spent her free time.

India knew things had to change, so she started to practise what she could say to Mary. Each day, she would plan to say something. Each day, she was too nervous. One lunch, India felt so sick with worry that she ran behind the sports shed to try and calm herself. Mary followed her and wanted to know what was going on. India knew this was the moment.

Taking a deep breath, India said, 'I feel like I'm not allowed to have friends other than you.'

'Yes, you are,' Mary interrupted. India gathered every bit of courage she could find, then looked Mary in the eye. 'When I play with someone else, you threaten to not be my friend. This makes me feel sad. Please stop doing this.' Mary's face reddened; tears welled up. She ran off, clearly distressed. India felt terrible for her friend, but she also felt like a weight had been lifted from her shoulders. She felt free.

And she was! She formed friendships with other kids. And a big, unexpected bonus? After the initial hurt, Mary learned that she needed to share friends. She learned that she didn't own anyone, and her best friends should be allowed to play with whomever they want.
India now skips to school. She has healthy friendships with kids who celebrate each other. When India shared this story with Grow Your Mind, she said the only thing she'd wished she'd done differently was speak up sooner. Because it not only helped her; it also helped Mary. Her parting words to us – and to you, dear reader – was this: don't put off hard conversations!

Listen to Grow Your Mind podcast episodes:
More Dangerous Than Smoking
Generous Assumptions

Also, head to our Grow Your Mind website, click on the *How to be a Good Enough Kid* page and get a free copy of the activities.

And to practise some of the ideas from this chapter, check out the following two pages.

CHALLENGE THE STORIES YOU TELL YOURSELF

Read the following prompts. Reflect on your initial gut reaction and then reframe your response with a generous assumption.

Your friends walk past you, whispering and giggling

Your friends catch up on the weekend without you

My teacher tells me off for talking in class

My parents nag me about having a clean room and taking a shower

My friend gets chosen for the part in the school play that I wanted

I don't get picked to be in the sports team

I walk into the classroom, and everyone looks up at me

I look at myself in the mirror

MAKE A NEW FRIEND BY ASKING ONE OF THESE QUESTIONS:

What sports or instruments do you play?

How many siblings or animals do you have?

If you could click your fingers and have food in your hands, what would it be?

Would you rather play games for a day or watch movies? Why?

What is a food you'd never eat, even if you hadn't eaten for three days?

Which subject do you like the best?

Would you rather never go to school or never celebrate Halloween again?

CREATE YOUR OWN RECIPE FOR A HEALTHY FRIENDSHIP

What core ingredients would be in it? Trust? Respect? Humour? What about the method for keeping it healthy? Sharing? Owning jealousy?

GIVE SOMEONE A COMPLIMENT

Sometimes asking questions can feel terrifying. If someone you admire does something well, tell them. Try these:

You have such nice handwriting
You play handball so well
You're amazing at ...

Get a bit quirky and try these!

You are stronger than the Hulk
You are faster than a gazelle fleeing a cheetah
Your drawing makes Picasso look like an amateur

Can you come up with four new compliments? Try using them this week.

1. ________________________________

2. ________________________________

3. ________________________________

4. ________________________________

CHAPTER 4: HOW TO MAKE UP YOUR MIND

(READ THIS OUT LOUD USING YOUR BEST ANIMAL VOICES)

PHEW. I KNOW YOU'RE MEANT TO BE WISE, BUT I WAS BEGINNING TO DOUBT IT.
SO, YOU CAN'T SEE THE THINGS I CAN SEE?
I THINK IT'S MY STRONG ABILITY TO FOCUS
DO YOU EVER CHANGE YOUR MIND?
ONCE I'VE MADE UP MY MIND, THAT'S IT. AND AFTER ALL, A DUCK IS A DUCK.
OH LOOK, IT'S A CAT WALKING BACKWARDS DOWN THE STEPS!
MMMM, OR UP?

HOW TO MAKE UP YOUR MIND

Once there were two dogs on either side of a fast-flowing river. They stood on the riverbank opposite their homes. It was too wide to jump across and the water was wild. Both could not make up their minds; should they stay on their side or try their luck flinging themselves to the other side? They sat in indecision for three days, starving. On the fourth day, one of the dogs grabbed a large, thin stick and threw it. It landed over the river, connecting the two banks. He wasn't certain the stick would bear his weight, so he insisted the other dog cross first. The other dog could see it was risky, and politely insisted that 'the one who throws the stick must walk across it first'. They sat, undecided, for three more days. By now, they were weak and malnourished. They came up with a plan: 'We have become so skinny, why don't we both cross at the same time?'

And so, they did. But when they met in the middle, despite being skin and bones, there was not enough room for them to pass each other. They sat, each insisting the other should walk backwards. Suddenly, there was a cracking noise. The stick snapped in two. The dogs fell into the wild river, never to be seen again.

AND THE POINT OF THAT DEPRESSING STORY IS?

Sometimes we make up our minds and stick to our guns so tightly that we end up suffering. We choose to be right over being flexible, kind or generous. And while it can be great to have strong opinions, beliefs and ideas, it's equally important to be open to having our views challenged.

Sometimes it can be super hard to make up our minds. We make decisions all day long – approximately 3000! By the time we're adults, we make 35,000 decisions a day.

Try making these decisions. Would you rather ...

- Be stuck in a cave with your soccer team for 17 days, or be adrift on a plank of wood in the ocean for five days on your own?
- Play cricket or touch footy this term?
- Eat Vegemite toast or Weetbix in the morning?
- Be mean to a kid and become popular, or be kind and lose friends?
- Do homework for the rest of your life, or go to school naked for a week?
- Lie to your best friend or get gastro?

Did you find these 'would you rather' questions tricky? Compare your answers with someone from your family. Why did you choose your answer, why did they choose theirs?

Decision-making is tricky. And after we finally make up our minds, we believe we're not allowed to change them. But the ability to change your mind means you have the capacity for flexible thinking*, which is a core mental fitness skill.

***Flexible thinking**

This is the ability to change our minds and cope with changing plans or disruptive life challenges. Flexible thinking is about being adaptable to situations while managing your reactions, even when it's challenging.

There are a lot of things that sway and influence our decisions; fortunately, there are a couple of great strategies you can use when making a choice. Scouts honour, I use these strategies myself.

ONE POWERFUL HABIT FOR MAKING DECISIONS

Before we go into this habit, think about what you might do in these scenarios:

1. Your friend asks you to hang out after school and ride bikes together, but you've signed up to violin this term, which you detest. Your mum and dad are both working, and you're meant to get yourself to the lesson. The temptation to ditch violin and hang with your friend is huge.

2. You're at the beach with your friends and your dad needs to go and pop some rubbish in the bin. He tells you to stay on the sand, out of the water. It's super hot and he's taking forever. One of your friends suggests you all go for a quick swim, outside the flags, because the safe swimming area is too crowded.

3. You find $1000 in cash on the way to the shops. Do you spend a bit of it, all of it or none of it? Do you tell someone you found it?

First things first: you don't need to make a decision straight away. Pause. Breathe in and out. If you can, splash your face with some water. Is there someone you can ask for advice? If not, ask yourself: am I breaking a rule by doing it?

Pause. Why all this pausing? Because the Wise Owl takes a while to warm up, especially if our Guard Dog is barking loudly. The Wise Owl needs to hear itself think! In fact, when your emotions are high, it's NOT a good idea to make a decision.

Next – and let's make this a lifelong habit – ask yourself: does this action match my values? Say what? If you were lost in a storm in the wilderness, you'd need a compass to guide you home. Values act in the same way. They guide you on what to do next. Values are what we choose our life to be about. Values are what we see as important. They're a guide for how we want to behave. You are going to feel lost without your values. If you don't know what's important to you, it's a recipe for following others blindly. Even if you have rockstar healthy friendships, you still want to make decisions that are true to you.

Living by your values will give you a strong sense of self. Not a fragile one. The difference? You'll lose games, face setbacks, stuff up and make big mistakes. You'll look around and see (or believe) that there are 'prettier' or 'smarter' people than you. With a fragile sense of self, you might conclude that you're not enough. Or you might be constantly preoccupied with what others think of you, which is actually none of your business!

With a strong sense of self, you're confident that you're behaving in a way that's true to you. You show up regularly in an honest, kind, helpful, generous, loving or brave way.

It's normal for values to change over time. When I was 18, my top value was adventure. These days, I value (cue cheesy music) love more than adventure. Knowing and living by your values can help you avoid unhealthy friendships. If a friend is consistently dishonest or ungenerous, you'll quickly pinpoint why things feel wrong – your values are clashing.

YOUR ANIMAL HELPER FOR THIS CHAPTER

WISE OWL

WHAT ARE YOUR VALUES?

It's a good idea to talk about it with your parents or the trusted adults who take care of you. Ask them about their values. Then ask them, 'What are our family's values?' Here are some examples to choose from:

CHOOSE YOUR VALUES:

Read through the list and ...

PLACE TWO TICKS BESIDE THE WORDS THAT ARE SUPER IMPORTANT TO YOU AND YOUR FAMILY.

✓✓

PLACE ONE TICK NEXT TO THE VALUES THAT ARE A LITTLE BIT IMPORTANT. LEAVE IT BLANK IF THE VALUE IS NOT MEANINGFUL TO YOU.

✓

OKAY, DONE? NOT YET? COME ON, HURRY UP! (PATIENCE IS CLEARLY NOT ONE OF MY VALUES.)

MY VALUES

Acceptance
Achievement
Adventure
Authenticity
Awe
Balance
Belonging
Cheerfulness
Community
Competition
Connection
Courage
Creativity
Curiosity
Dependability
Determination
Diversity
Environment
Efficiency
Empathy
Equality
Excellence
Fairness
Faith
Family
Fitness
Friendship
Fun
Generosity
Giving back
Grace
Gratitude
Growth
Happiness
Health
Honesty
Hope
Humility
Humour
Inclusion
Independence
Integrity
Joy
Kindness
Learning
Love
Loyalty
Making a difference
Mindfulness
Nature
Openness
Optimism
Order
Passion
Peace
Power
Relaxation
Reliability
Religion
Reputation
Resilience
Respect
Safety
Self-control
Self-expression
Self-respect
Service
Spirituality
Sportsmanship
Teamwork
Time
Trust

NOW, LOOK AT THE VALUES WHERE THERE ARE TWO TICKS NEXT TO THEM. CIRCLE THE FOUR MOST IMPORTANT ONES.

Woah! That groan was audible from cow-loving Jamberoo. I can hear you saying – 'But I have 22 words with two ticks, how can I get it down to four?' Are you telling me that I have to sacrifice 'love' over 'kindness' in the pursuit of your ridiculous and irrational demands?

Take a chill pill, calm your farm. (You know how to do that now.) You HAVE to get it down to four and here's why: let's rewind to that scenario where your mates asked you to swim outside the flags. You say to them – 'Just a second' – and ask yourself, 'Is this in line with my 22 values?!' Too tricky. Get it down to four. Put your values down in the shape of a compass. Our values at Grow Your Mind are the ones below. What about you?

NOW YOU KNOW YOUR VALUES, YOU'LL NEVER STRUGGLE WITH A DECISION, RIGHT?

Wrong. Sorry. Knowing your values is super helpful. It's easy to listen to your values and say 'no' to your brother or sister. But what about the most popular kid at school? What about a teacher? Or a sports coach? What if they ask you to do something that makes you feel uncomfortable and it's not in line with your values? Saying 'no' is actually really tricky.

Again, pause. If the word 'no' is too terrifying, or you're worried about letting someone down, here are some other ways to say 'no':

Not today

I'm not so sure

I'll have a think about it

I need to go now, but I'll get back to you

Not this time

I don't feel comfortable

My parents said no

Plus, these ones:

I'd love to, but I can't

I think I'll pass

It's not really my thing, but thanks

Maybe next time

I appreciate the invitation, but I'm completely booked

Thanks for thinking of me, but I can't

You're so kind to think of me, but I can't

You can also totally blame your parents:

My mum and dad would be furious. They'd make my life as painful as cutting up onions without goggles.

Remember, you might say 'yes' to something, but you can always change your mind at any time. These are the principles of something called 'consent'. Consent means you give permission for something to happen. And just like friendship, there are golden rules for consent. Yumi Stynes and Melissa Kang are two incredible humans who have an awesome book called *Welcome to Consent*. In their book, they outline the following golden rules of consent:

Here's an example of these rules in action:

> One afternoon, you give enthusiastic permission (without peer pressure) for your best friend to walk your dog. She rocks up the next day and tries to take your dog without asking (breaking the 'consent needs to be specific' rule). She then demands you give her the dog or she'll never talk to you again (breaking the 'consent should be enthusiastic and freely given' rule). You nod but feel uncomfortable. She walks away and, in the nick of time, you become a part-time member of The Supremes and sing: 'STOP! In the name of consent ... I want my dog back. Think it over'. Your friend says, 'Too bad – you said yes', (breaking the 'consent can change' rule). Your friend is such a rule breaker, BTW. If you value respect, you and your friends have a value clash happening here.

WHAT IF YOU ARE THE ONE ASKING?

Most of us don't love hearing the word 'no'. It doesn't fill our hearts with joy. Some of us are, however, better at receiving a 'no' than others. For some, a 'no' sucks. For others, a 'no' is an insult. This is something you need to work on. Being a good enough kid has a few prerequisites, and respecting other people's boundaries is compulsory criteria.

WHEN YOU HEAR A NO TRY THIS:

1. TAKE A DEEP BREATH

2. NOTICE WHAT YOU ARE FEELING AND WHERE

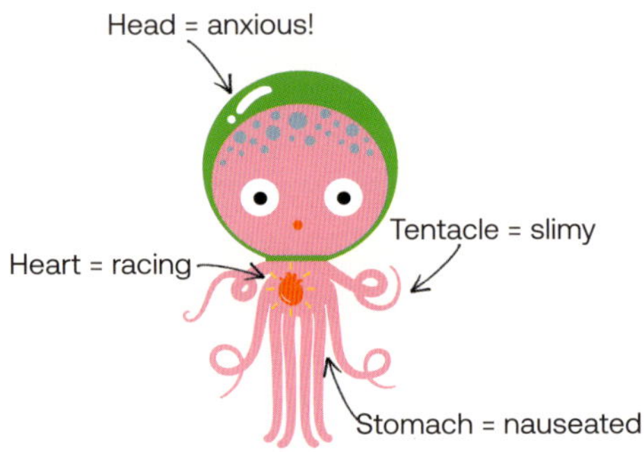

3. REMIND YOURSELF THIS BIG FEELING WON'T LAST

4. IT'S NORMAL TO FEEL UPSET WHEN YOU HEAR A 'NO', BUT THAT DOES NOT MEAN YOU GET TO ACT IN A RUDE, THREATENING OR AGGRESSIVE MANNER!

Remember:

- It's okay to not always get your way
- You can make up your mind and change it

HOW TO MAKE A GOOD DECISION

PERMISSION TO BE HUMAN AND GOOD ENOUGH

You will make bad decisions. The prefrontal cortex (your Wise Owl) is the last part of the brain to fully develop. So be kind to yourself, you are a work in progress. You also have full permission to change your mind. You might form opinions and express them to others. This is great. Try not to get too stuck in your opinion. It's not about being 'wrong', it's about saying to someone, 'You made me think differently about that'. The Wise Owl was all over this in the art gallery with the Sifting Sooty, but the Sifting Sooty would not move from his opinion. Your sense of self and your self-worth should not be tied to being right. When you're really stuck on what to do next, think about your values. Which direction are they pointing you in?

BRAIN BREAK:

What animal am I?

I have 'Pink Fairy' at the start of my name. I know, it's tough to be taken seriously. The other part of my name in Spanish means 'little armoured one'. I'm tiny and a proud tunneller, which means I live underground. I have soft fur, a tail and relatively large feet.

Share these facts with someone near you. Do they have any others to add?

The water in your glass was formed billions of years ago in space.

Your blood is 75% water.

Your poop is also 75% water.

SHINE THE SPOTLIGHT ON ...

AUSTRALIAN SIKH VOLUNTEERS:

IN SERVICE OF HUMANITY

Australian Sikh Volunteers is a charity that focuses on reducing distress in the community by providing FREE FOOD to disadvantaged and needy individuals and families.

"Just be nice. Be nice to everyone. Speak with passion, speak politely."
Jaswinder Singh

Research Challenge: Okay, good enough kid, see what you can find out about the Australian Sikh volunteers. Why do you think we've included them in this chapter? Hint: values!

THE EASTER SHOW DILEMMA: RAJI AND ZARA'S STORY

Raji and her friend Zara were thrilled to go to the Easter Show. They walked dogs all summer holidays to save enough money for the entry ticket, the rides and a showbag. The day arrived and the girls rushed into the showground. Zara insisted they go on the Gravitron, a ride that spins so fast you end up being stuck to the wall with your feet in the air. Raji was adamant that she didn't want to do this:

'It'll make me sick!', Raji cried.

'You can't quit on me now; we're doing the show together!', Zara retorted, grabbing Raji's hand and dragging her toward the ride.

When the ride finished, Raji rushed to the nearest tree and vomited. As she bent over, hurling her guts out, her backpack tipped and $20 fell out. Time slowed down for Zara. She stared at the $20. She already had $20, but if she had $40, she could get more showbags. The temptation was too great. With one hand on Raji's back, soothing her friend, she picked up the $20 with her other hand and pocketed it.

Raji sat up, finally feeling better, and suggested they go and get their showbag. The girls raced to the pavilion to see their options. Raji decided on the Tim Tam showbag. It was $18. When she went to pay, she couldn't find her money! She tore open her backpack, looking for her money in every possible place, flinging the contents of her bag onto the ground. But it was gone. Zara felt sick, but she thought it was too late to come clean. Raji put on a brave front and said she'd wait outside until Zara finished.

Zara's nausea turned into excitement. Her $40 could get her the Tim Tam showbag and the Cadbury Favourites showbag. She had $2 change, so she bought Raji the Bertie Beetle bag with one solitary chocolate inside. Zara hid the Cadbury Favourites inside the Tim Tam showbag and went outside.

Raji was super thankful for the Bertie Beetle showbag and Zara's sick feeling returned. They rode the train home together and Zara could not bring herself to talk to her friend or look her in the eye. Raji eventually asked, 'Can I see what's in your Tim Tam showbag?'

'No, it's mine,' Zara said, snatching it away.

An awkward silence fell. Raji was bewildered. Zara knew she'd made the wrong decision. She also knew that honesty was the value she and Raji had always shared. When they arrived at her stop, she stood up and abruptly tossed her showbags at Raji.

'I'm so sorry!', she shouted, bolting off the train. Raji was utterly confused. She looked into the showbag and it dawned on her. Zara stood on the station platform and peered through the window as the doors of the train closed. She saw her friend's face fall. She knew their friendship was over.

But guess what? It wasn't over. Zara gave Raji space and time. Slowly, they built up trust again. Years later, Zara asked Raji, 'Why did you forgive me?'

'How do you know I really have?!', Raji replied with a twinkle in her eyes. 'In my culture, forgiveness is a really important value. It actually made me feel lighter, letting go of my hurt. Plus, I knew you were truly sorry.' Zara reached out to hold her friend's hand, and Raji quickly added: 'But now, when I go to the show, I keep my money zipped up!'

Listen to Grow Your Mind podcast episodes:
Lost in the Woods
Values (Song)

Also, head to our Grow Your Mind website, click on the *How to be a Good Enough Kid* page and get a free copy of the activities.

And to practise some of the ideas from this chapter, check out below and the page opposite.

ASK A TRUSTED ADULT THESE QUESTIONS:

- Have you ever found it really hard to make a decision? What helped?
- Have you ever made a decision that seemed super bad, but ended up being a good one?
- Do you know what your four key values are? How do these help you?
- Have you ever found it hard to say 'no' to someone? What did you do?
- Is there a time in your life when someone forgave you, even if you didn't deserve it? Do you think it helped?
- Does your current hobby match your values?

REAL SCENARIOS: WHAT WOULD YOU DO?

- You're excellent at swimming. The swimming carnival arrives, and you've won four out of the five races you're competing in. It's time for the final race. Your best friend asks you to go slow so he can win. What do you do? Why?
- It's time to apply for a leadership role in Year 6. A lot of people have told you that you'd make an excellent house captain, including several teachers. You go to a religious school and on the application form they ask you about your faith. You don't really believe in any of it. You know that if you say this, there's a high chance you won't be selected. What do you do? Why?
- You're asked to go to a friend's place to hang out. When you got there, they steal $10 from their dad's wallet. They get caught. Their dad is scary and tough on your friend, so your mate says it was your idea. You know his dad won't get mad at you. What do you do? Why?

CHAPTER 5:
HOW TO DIG YOURSELF OUT OF A HOLE

(READ THIS OUT LOUD USING
YOUR BEST ANIMAL VOICES)

SURE. THE THING IS, YOUR APOLOGY SHOULD BE AN APOLOGY, NOT A JUSTIFICATION.
JUSTIFICATION, I LIKE THE WORD, I NEED TO REMEMBER IT.
OK I'M SORRY. LET'S BE BEST FRIENDS, OK? TIME TO GET OVER IT.
WHAT? WHY ARE YOU STILL SULKING?
A GOOD APOLOGY SHOULDN'T REQUIRE ME TO DO ANYTHING
ARRGGHHH YOU ARE MAKING ME FURIOUS
I AM NEVER TALKING TO YOU AGAIN
AND YOUR SPECIES IS RESPONSIBLE FOR THE DEATH OF 377 MILLION BIRDS A YEAR!
THAT'S OVER ONE MILLION BIRDS A DAY
NO APOLOGY FROM YOU WOULD EVER MAKE UP FOR THAT!
I'M VEGAN!

HOW TO DIG YOURSELF OUT OF A **HOLE**

Have you ever regretted saying something in a moment of anger? It's a bit like asking, 'Have you ever done a wee?' We all have. We all lose our cool and say things we regret. So ... what do you do after your mouth explosion? How do you move on when you've been wronged? How does the cat recover from being told its species is responsible for 377 million birds dying each year? It's going to be tough!

As always, it's okay to feel what you feel. It's not okay to act in a way that scares or hurts other people. And yet we all do it. Luckily, there's power in something called 'repair'. This is when we own our behaviour and admit that we wish we'd done things differently. Repair can really save a relationship. The thing is, most of us don't do the repair part very well. We often put a 'but' in our apologies, and we quickly turn to rage if people don't forgive us straight away. And then we find ourselves deep in a hole with no shovel to dig our way out, surrounded by a whole heap of self-righteousness*.

***Self-righteousness**

The belief that your views and values are more important and morally better than someone else's.

This is a tricky place to be. In fact, it would be easier to get yourself out of a big sinkhole in the ground. But never fear, I've got a few tools to throw down to you. Try them out. See what works.

Sometimes we find ourselves in the kind of hole where we did or said the wrong thing, but we feel too ashamed to admit it. We're in a shame hole. And that's a miserable, unhelpful place to be. We feel really bad when we experience shame, but we're also super quick to blame others. We flip from thinking, 'It's all my fault', to taking no responsibility for what we've done. For example, 'I feel so bad for lying to you, I'm such a horrible person.' One second pause. 'But you can be really difficult and mean too.'

Shame loves hiding out, so you need to get a shovel and dig and dig and dig up to a spot where the light creeps in. Shame will start to lose its power out in the sun.
A bit like vampires.
And snowmen. And ice cream.

How do we climb out of the hole of self-righteousness or shame?

You need your Elephant (the hippocampus), which works super well with sleep. Let's face it, it's easier to overcome most challenges if we've slept well. Without sleep, we can behave like tall toddlers. This makes getting out of the hole very difficult.

YOUR ANIMAL HELPER FOR THIS CHAPTER

REMEMBER, WE *CAN* GET OUT OF A HOLE

I've got five ideas for getting yourself out of a hole. Let's call each idea a 'shovel'. Some of these shovels might be the motivation you need to start digging. Others are about how to do the digging.

LET IT GO

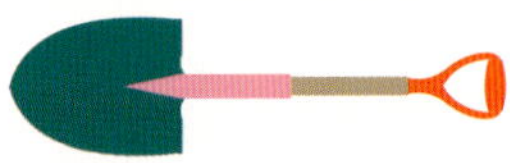

If you have the choice between being right or being kind, which one will you choose? What would it look like if you stopped being angry about a situation? If you're truly right and an injustice has occurred, will this be a big issue in five days? Five months? Five years? If the answer is 'no', let it go!

Let's say you have a fight with your friend, and you refuse to speak to them for a few days. What do you care more about – repairing the friendship or guarding your hurt? Only you can answer this. But I'd guess, if you really stopped and asked yourself this question, you'd choose to dig your way out and repair the relationship.

Grudges can feel powerful to hold onto. But it's a false power. Don't worry, your Elephant may never forget the hurt, but you can let go of the hold it has on you.

DEEP BREATHS

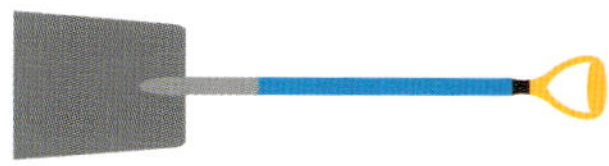

It's going to be nearly impossible to make good decisions if you don't give yourself a chance to calm down and finish your stress response cycle. Taking some deep, calming breaths will stop your Guard Dog from barking so loudly. You could try belly breathing. Lie down and notice your belly rising and falling as you take five slow, deep breaths. Or you could trace your hand with a few rounds of finger breathing (see page 58).

COUNT

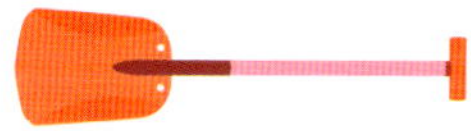

It's super helpful to give your Wise Owl (the prefrontal cortex) time to come up with a good plan. Counting before you react will give you that time. The pause will allow your Wise Owl to problem solve and work out a helpful response to the issue. And it probably knows where the shovel is so you can start digging. But you need your Elephant to remind you to do the counting in the first place. You can count to ten and back down again a few times.

REHEARSE

This might feel a bit strange, but practise what you might say to the person. You could write it down, say it in your head or even share it with someone you trust. Start with 'I' and 'when' sentences: 'I feel sad when you ignore me' or 'I felt angry when I didn't get my way.' Then name the behaviour and explain that you wish you'd behaved differently. It might sound like this: 'I wish I hadn't yelled and called you a poo-poo-brain-fart-face, that was a mean and untrue thing to say. I'm sorry.' You need to practise it. Remember, practice makes progress. And if you say sorry, keep any 'buts' out of it!

Now I want to introduce you to Julia Baird. Julia has written lots of books that I devour and reread. One of them is about something called 'grace'. Grace is being kind when no one is looking. It's forgiving someone without being pressured to do so. It's helping someone who will never repay you. It's a combination of generosity, compassion and empathy. It's seeing the best in someone, even when they're driving you nuts. Remember golden friendship rule #5?

5

Generous assumptions help every friendship. What is the best you could assume about your friend?

GRACE

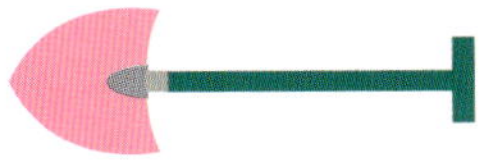

It's where we aim to let go of a grudge. This can be hard to do when someone is being incredibly irritating. Grace, our trusty shovel, knows that everyone is capable of being a little vexing*; we're all flawed AND we are more than our mistakes. Our reliable shovel, Grace, knows that it's hard to move on, but it's also hard to hold onto anger. Forgiving someone or letting go of a grudge is not weak. In fact, Julia Baird says: 'It requires grit and strength'.

***Vexing**

Bothersome, infuriating, maddening!

THE SHOVELLING ISN'T WORKING. WHAT CAN YOU DO?

Staying in the hole happens a lot when you argue with friends. These arguments could be massive fights or tense moments where we feel hurt or wish we felt in control. First up, please remember that it's normal and healthy to disagree and have conflict with our friends. Here are some quick facts about conflict to remember (tell your Elephant to store these in your long-term memory):

Conflict is a normal and healthy part of any relationship

We can deal with conflict in harmful or helpful ways

Having a calm Guard Dog keeps conflict helpful

Your Sensitive Octopus helps you be empathetic and imagine another perspective

Helpful things you can do after a fight with a friend:

- Go outside
- Do something creative
- Lie down and listen to music
- Move your body
- Sleep!
- Splash your face with cold water
- Walk away
- Think of a strength that might help you

GROW A LITTLE PERSPECTIVE

It's super tricky to imagine another person's point of view when you're angry. Have you ever played handball and you were CERTAIN the ball was out, yet your buddy was 100% positive it was on the line? This might have made you feel extremely mad and think bad things about your friend. Can you see how this handball example is related to the image below?

Growing perspective takes practice. Consider a fallen tree in the forest: to us, it may look like rotten, useless wood. But what about the insects who love living in the log? To them, it's a safe haven of food, family and important work. And how about the insect-eating echidna who reaps the benefits of this situation? It's not necessarily about working out what is wrong and right. Instead, it's about understanding different perspectives before you make decisions. Practise now. Switch on your Elephant and recall a recent argument you had with someone. Now, tell it from their perspective. What were they thinking? What were they feeling? What do you think they saw, heard or noticed? This will feel hard to do. But it's a skill for life. And remember, practice makes ... progress!

TALK IT OUT TO GET OUT (OF THE HOLE)

Are you ready to talk it out?
Conflict, awkward moments, misunderstandings: these are a normal part of any friendship. Talking it out can help when we feel hurt or angry with a friend.

Is your Guard Dog calm?

- NO → **That's ok!** **Take 3 deep breaths.** Splash your face with cold water.

  What character strengths might help you in this conversation?

  Remember: **Clear is kind (use tact), unclear is unkind.** If you can't talk to your friend, don't speak about that person behind their back.

- YES → Can you talk about it without involving others?

Can you talk about it without involving others?

- NO → (see "That's ok!" above)
- YES → Can you start the conversation with *I feel ... When you ...* Or *I wish ...*

Can you start the conversation with *I feel ...* *When you ...* Or *I wish ...*

- NO → Practice makes progress. Start practising.
- YES → Are you open to coming up with solutions together?

Are you open to coming up with solutions together?

- NO → You aren't quite ready! Move your body, have a drink and wait until your Guard Dog is open to problem solving.
- YES → If you start talking and it gets mean or unhelpful, can you ask to take a break and try again later?

If you start talking and it gets mean or unhelpful, can you ask to take a break and try again later?

- NO → Practise, practise, practise until you *can* do it!
- YES → **You are ready, may the force be with you!**

CAN'T I JUST SAY SORRY?

Sort of. And sort of not. We all tend to suck at saying sorry. We say things like:

1. I'm sorry I yelled, but you were being so annoying.
2. I'm sorry I ignored you, but I was tired, and you were so frustrating.
3. I'm sorry, best friends again?
4. I'm sorry, now let's get over it.
5. I'm sorry you're upset by this.

You might think you're digging your way out of the hole, but all these apologies are flawed. The first two include 'but'. And remember, it's important to keep that three-letter word out of your apology. Just like the cat said to the elephant, apologies should be 'but'-free. Why? Because you think you're being the bigger person by apologising, yet you're actually just excusing your behaviour. You need to talk about how you feel and what you wish had been different, then take responsibility for your part, with no 'but.'

The third and fourth apologies are pretty rubbish because they're asking for something. A good apology asks for nothing in return. And finally, the fifth is my least favourite apology. It's not even an apology. You're essentially saying that the problem lies with the person and their reaction; it's nothing you did. For example, imagine your younger sister was playing with a ball inside. She throws the ball, and it lands right on top of the Lego masterpiece you've been working on for weeks. You're furious. She shrugs her shoulders and says, 'Sorry you're so upset.' She walks away. How would that leave you feeling? It's not much of an apology, is it?

Learning to let go, give a good apology and make amends with someone you care about is the BEST way to get yourself out of a hole. We can take inspiration from Dr Harriet Lerner, a psychologist who's authored 12 books, including one about apologising. Try using these steps in the sorry flow chart.

ARE YOU READY TO SAY SORRY?

SLEEP ON IT!

If I've behaved badly and I'm in a shame hole, I tell myself to sleep on it. It's a funny expression. Sleep on what, exactly? If I try and sleep on my dilemma, does that mean I'm going to spend the night tossing and turning, still thinking about it? Probably. So, here's what I recommend. Put a notepad beside your bed. If you're in a dark hole of shame or self-righteousness, or you're just super hurt and mad, write everything down. Everything. Then tell the notepad: 'This is your job. Remember all these things so I can sleep. I'll take over in the morning.' And then go to sleep. The next morning, wake up, get the notepad, have a quick read and then rip out the page and dispose of it. These words are about things we felt stuck on; we wouldn't necessarily want to say them aloud as they aren't terribly helpful.

You'll find sleep makes everything feel more manageable and hopeful. The Elephant (your hippocampus) loves sleep. During snooze time, it organises and processes memories, and if you learned something interesting or important that day, it can help you master it WHILE YOU SLEEP! After a good sleep, our mood improves. Our ability to problem solve improves. The world looks better. Our Elephant reminds us of all the times we've come unstuck. It will help us let go of the need to be right and choose kindness instead. Sleep is our strongest and most reliable shovel.

BRAIN BREAK:

What is this invertebrate?

It aerates and mixes the soil, making it richer in nutrients. Charles Darwin (who studied nature and came up with a theory of evolution) once wrote about this ear-less creature: 'It may be doubted whether there are many other animals which have played so important a part in the history of the world, as have these lowly organised creatures.'

Share this fact:

There is a snake that has adapted its tail to resemble a spider. They do this to attract birds who think they are chasing a spider – until it's too late!

SHINE THE SPOTLIGHT ON ...

STEVE SMITH:

AUSTRALIAN CRICKETER + SPEAKER

> *"I'll do everything I can to make up for my mistake and the damage it has caused ... If any good can come from this, if there is a lesson for others, I hope I can be a force for change."*

Research Challenge: Find out why we've spotlighted Steve Smith. How did he dig himself out of the shame hole he created?

THE PHOTO DELETE – LACHIE'S STORY

Lachie's sister and dad returned from a day at the zoo together, and Lachie was furious. His parents had started this tradition of taking each of them, alone, to somewhere they loved. Lachie picked ten-pin bowling, which only went for an hour. His sister got a whole day with his dad. *Life is so unfair*, Lachie sulked.

Lachie's dad was showing photos from the day. There was one with his sister and a seal, and a selfie of the two of them with a giraffe. Lachie felt nauseated by their enthusiasm. They got up to grab a snack and, in a fit of rage, Lachie took his dad's phone and deleted every photo from their day. He turned the phone off and hid it down the side of the sofa.

A moment later, his mum walked into the room and wanted to see the photos. They searched for the phone for an hour. Lachie felt incredibly nervous, but he was still sure that what he'd done was right. I mean, where were all the photos of him from ten-pin bowling? NOWHERE!

Lachie's dad was sure the phone had been on the sofa, so he started to pull out the cushions. Lachie's heart was racing. A moment later, his dad found the phone. He looked confused, why was it turned off? He began searching for the photos, saying, 'I don't get it, where are they?'

'I hate you all!', Lachie shouted, his anxiety turning to anger. 'You love her more than me. I'm LEAVING.'

Lachie ran out of the room, out of the house and down the street. He hid under a tree and made plans to run away for good. As he sat there, fuming, he kept thinking, *stupid family, selfish family – it's SO unfair!*

But then Lachie started to feel confused. He felt so much anger towards them, but he was also feeling really bad about himself. Was it fair to delete the photos? *YES*.

Was it *really* fair, though? *Crap. Crap. Crap*.

It dawned on Lachie that perhaps he'd gone too far. But what was he going to do now? In his mind there was no way he could EVER return home. But where could he go? Maybe he could make a living from ten-pin bowling – or destroying evidence of crimes?

Lachie knew he needed a better plan with more robust career aspirations. He also thought about his dog and his fish and how much he'd miss them. He realised he needed to face the music. He took some big deep breaths and started walking back home.

When he arrived, it was clear his sister had been crying. His parents didn't look angry. It was so much worse – they looked disappointed! Lachie desperately wanted his sister to say horrible things or his parents to yell at him. But everyone was quiet and sad. Lachie really wanted to tell them all the things they had done wrong. But instead, he took another big deep breath and said: 'Well, this is awkward.'

More silence. He'd have to do better.

'I'm so sorry. That was a selfish and awful thing to do.'

It wasn't a magic spell moment. They didn't break into laughter or hug each other. But over the next few days, Lachie tried to be extra helpful. He made his sister cookies. He wrote her a note and spent his pocket money on a magazine he knew she wanted. And with time, she really did forgive Lachie.

Listen to Grow Your Mind podcast episodes: *Keep it But Free*

Also, head to our Grow Your Mind website, click on the *How to be a Good Enough Kid* page and get a free copy of the activities.

And to practise some of the ideas from this chapter, check out below and the page opposite.

WHICH SHOVEL CAN YOU PRACTISE USING THIS WEEK?

Is there a hurt you're holding onto? How can you let go of it?

____

____

Practise using 'When' and 'I' statements during conflict. For example, instead of saying, 'You've been mean behind my back, that makes me so angry', try: 'When you say mean things about me behind my back, I feel angry.' Please note, sometimes doing this can feel scary or awkward. An alternative option is to say what you wish for. For example: 'I wish you didn't say mean things behind my back.'

REWRITE THESE SENTENCES USING EITHER 'WHEN' AND 'I' OR 'WISH':

You always leave me out, it's so unfair.

____

____

____

You haven't talked to me all day, why do you have to be so horrible to me?

____

____

____

You always get your way, it's not okay for you to be like this.

____

____

____

CHAPTER 6:
HOW TO BE BRAVE WHEN YOU ARE TERRIFIED

(READ THIS OUT LOUD USING YOUR BEST ANIMAL VOICES)

ARE YOU TRYING TO GET OUT OF THE EVENT?
NO
YES
WHY? YOU WERE BEST IN SHOW LAST YEAR
THIS IS YOUR TIME TO SHINE
THIS IS MY TIME TO FAIL. I CAN'T DO IT. TO GO FROM CHAMPION TO LAST PLACE.
YOU WON'T COME LAS—
LOSER!
I'M NOT DOING IT. GRRRRRRRRRRRRR
THE RACE ISN'T A THREAT
GRRRRRRRRRRRRRRR
IT'S A CHALLENGE

HOW TO BE BRAVE WHEN YOU ARE TERRIFIED

The day has come for you to try out for a performing arts high school. You need to submit an art portfolio and deliver a speech about why you would be an asset to the school. But you're struck down with a super sore tummy. It feels like you can't move. You tell your parents you need to cancel.

Instead of following your clear instructions, your parents tell you about your Guard Dog (the amygdala). They tell you it's trying to protect you from danger, but there's no danger in delivering a speech. You look at them as though they're mad. This is NOT the time to be talking about Guard Dogs. Plus, you take offence that they're accusing you of being anxious, when you clearly need to lie down, under your doona, with Netflix and a block of chocolate.

They keep talking. They say there's nothing wrong with anxiety; it doesn't mean your brain is broken. Instead, your brain is trying really hard to do its job, but it can't always tell the difference between real and perceived danger. Instead of protecting you, your brain *overprotects* you in a way that's not necessary or helpful.

Urgh, you think. Does this mean I still have to go? Sore tummy and all?

YOUR ANIMAL HELPER FOR THIS CHAPTER

GUARD DOG

Your brain is incredible, but it needs you to be the boss, especially when it perceives a threat. You can help your Guard Dog chill by asking it the magic question:

**Is this a threat,
a challenge
or an opportunity?**

I learned to ask this question thanks to Dr Sarah McKay, a neuroscientist and advisor to Grow Your Mind. This question teaches our Guard Dog to tell the difference between what is, according to anxiety expert and author, Karen Young, 'scary dangerous' or 'scary safe'. It also means we can be brave when we're terrified. Because we can let our brain know that being scared and being brave go hand in hand.

Take me, for instance. I surf on Fridays with a group of women who are really good at surfing, but my Guard Dog goes into threat mode. I find the ocean terrifying. I'm sure I'm going to be crushed by a wave or taken out to sea. But I think what is really happening is this: I go into threat mode because it's hard to be the worst at something. But the magic question (is it a threat, challenge or opportunity?) helps me every Friday.

I realise that surfing is an opportunity for me to show compassion for others who may be less confident at doing things I find easy. Surfing is a challenge, it teaches me to keep trying, even when my nose is full of salt water and my hair has more sand in it than the Sahara.

DEFINING THREATS, CHALLENGES AND OPPORTUNITIES

IS THIS A THREAT?

You are in danger or risk of serious harm

IS THIS A CHALLENGE?

You are being tested or have a problem to face (no danger)

IS THIS AN OPPORTUNITY?

You might learn something new from this situation or grow as a person (no danger)

THE GUARD DOG'S SECRET SKILL

Remember how your Elephant (the hippocampus) plays a crucial role in memory? Well, the Guard Dog does too. That's why it's so important to ask the question: is this a threat, challenge or opportunity?

Take trying a new food that's spicy or different – is eating it a threat, challenge or opportunity? If you deal with it as a threat, then you never get a chance to explore and learn. But if you and your Guard Dog decide it's a challenge or an opportunity to try something new, then the next time you face something similar (like Pad Thai, Nasi Goreng or spring rolls), your Guard Dog will know you're not in danger. If you go to a holiday camp and you don't know anyone, it might take a while to convince your Guard Dog to see this as an opportunity to make new friends. But if you smile and participate in the activities, your Guard Dog will realise that these kinds of social situations are safe.

Instead of going into threat mode (avoiding, refusing, yelling or fighting) the Guard Dog will *remember* that you're feeling uncomfortable because it's a challenge or an opportunity. This will save you a lot of heartache, tantrums and refusals. It also means that you are stretching yourself to do things that are scary, but safe.

YOUR TURN!

Here are some scenarios. Grab a partner or a trusted adult and decide if a scenario is a threat, a challenge or an opportunity.

YOU ARE ASKED TO DELIVER A SPEECH IN ASSEMBLY ABOUT CLIMATE CHANGE

YOUR FRIEND SHARES A SECRET ABOUT WHO YOU HAVE A CRUSH ON

IT'S YOUR FIRST DAY AT A NEW SCHOOL AND YOU DON'T KNOW ANYONE

YOU ARE ASKED TO SIT AN EXAM FOR AN EXTENSION CLASS

YOUR OLDER COUSIN TOUCHES YOU IN A WAY THAT FEELS UNCOMFORTABLE AND ASKS YOU NOT TO TELL ANYONE*

*Remember – not all secrets should be kept. Always tell a trusted adult if you feel unsafe.

TRY A POSITIVE AFFIRMATION

Despite doing all the mindful breathing a young person can do, the threat mode is still not shifting. In fact, mindful breathing is now making you feel more anxious and terrified. If you're told to take one more big deep breath you might turn into Nick Kyrgios when he loses a point in tennis (look him up). There are other options that are totally good enough for a good enough kid like you. For example, no amount of box breathing or finger breathing will help me get in the ocean alone with my surfboard. But what does help is a positive affirmation. An affirmation is something we say to ourselves; it can be negative or positive. For example, 'I'm hopeless' vs 'I've got this – I can do hard things.' Here are ten positive affirmations you can use when your body is stuck in threat mode:

I can be brave and scared at the same time.

I can do hard things.

I am doing the best I can.

It's scary safe, not scary dangerous. I've got this.

Breathe in, breathe out. I can do this.

I am stronger than I feel.

I can, I will, I am.

I am wired for this.

Today, I choose to say 'yes'.

I am loved; I am safe.

STILL STUCK IN THREAT MODE?

HERE ARE FIVE IDEAS TO PRACTISE GETTING UNSTUCK:

MOVE YOUR BODY

You've heard me suggest it before: move your body every single day. Just get into the habit now. When you feel super stressed, angry or worried – move your body. When you are happy, calm or joyful – move your body. Find the way you like to move it and do it. When you're stuck in threat mode, moving your body will create a flood of endorphins (those feel-good hormones). This will help change you from a problem seeker to a problem solver.

CREATE SOMETHING

I find drawing stick-figures challenging. We often avoid art because we think we aren't 'good' at it – especially if our friends have incredible artistic skills. It's easy to feel a little self-conscious about sketching when you're sitting beside the next Van Gogh or Banksy. With all due respect to ultra-talented artists, I don't believe us stick-figure drawers should hang up our crayons. Instead, we should all create for the sake of creating.

When we are creative, we get an increase in dopamine (a neurotransmitter that boosts mood, focus and ability to cope with stress). Having a creative outlet, whether it be making a stone statue, cooking up a delicious meal, painting, collaging or putting together a photo book, is a

brilliant thing for our mental health. It helps our brain feel safe and gets us out of threat mode.

READ

It does not matter if you think a book is too young for you. If you like it, read it. Picture books are packed with meaning and lessons for life. Find the thing that YOU like to read. Read something for joy, because it sparks curiosity or because it's an escape.

Reading calms us down, reduces our stress levels and allows our brains to have a break from our current reality.

WRITE ABOUT IT

This strategy is great when you're in a shame hole, but it also helps when you're in threat mode. Writing down what you're worried about gives you a little bit of distance from the problem. Get it all out. Swear if you need to. Then scrunch it up. Destroy the evidence before your folks or carers see it.

SHAKE IT OFF

Whether you are sitting or standing, shake your body or tap your face and shoulders.

Just start shaking one foot, then the other. Shake your calves, your knees and work your way up each side of your body. Our bodies were meant to move, but we can get stuck and our emotions can too. Give your body a pat on the arms, legs, shoulders and gently on the head. Anything to get you out of threat mode.

The important thing is practice makes ... progress. Every time you choose to be brave and do something that is safe but scary, you get a little more out of life. Your Guard Dog will remember that you can be brave.

BRAIN BREAK:

What animal am I?

I'm one of the most venomous animals in the world. My head is the size of a golf ball. You will know when I'm in threat mode as my blue rings will appear and start to pulsate! Run for your life when this happens as I pack enough venom to kill 25 humans.

Share these facts tonight at the dinner table:

Male capuchins (monkeys) urinate in their hands and use their urine to wash their feet*.

Male gentoo penguins offer rocks as gifts to females they want to impress.

*Remind your Elephant: never shake hands with a male capuchin.

SHINE THE SPOTLIGHT ON ...

ADAM GOODES:

PROUD ADNYAMATHANHA/NARUNGGA MAN, FORMER AFL STAR + TOTAL LEGEND

"The best thing that I did was get myself out of an environment that was toxic to me and to my mental health. That was through retiring from football."

Research Challenge: How did the Australian public react to Adam Goodes calling out racism? Did they see it as a threat, challenge or an opportunity?

SCHOOL CAMP ISN'T LIFE-THREATENING – MÙCHÉN'S STORY

Mùchén was a popular, smart, sporty and musical kid. In Year 5, life changed dramatically for Mùchén. He was away at music camp when his beloved dad died suddenly of a brain aneurysm. One day he was there, a strong figure in his life, kind and funny. The next day, he'd disappeared forever.

On the outside, Mùchén seemed okay. He went to school, participated in all the activities, kept up the jokes and made people feel relaxed. But on the inside, Mùchén was heartbroken. He longed to see his dad, he longed to change the past. He noticed small changes in himself. He didn't want to go to anyone's house for hangouts or sleepovers anymore. He could feel his heart racing when people asked him to come over and he would quickly come up with an excuse. Year 6 camp was looming, something that Mùchén used to look forward to. Now the thought of it would make him feel sick.

Mùchén planned to fake an illness. He approached his mum and said his back and stomach hurt and he couldn't go to camp. She tried to encourage him, but Mùchén grew more distressed. He shouted at her and slammed his bedroom door.

Mùchén's mum was a bit of a legend. She gently knocked on his door and told him that if he wanted to tell her the real reason he didn't want to go to camp, she was ready to listen. Mùchén couldn't explain his fear. He just felt in his body that something would go horribly wrong. He had learned about asking whether something was a threat, challenge or opportunity. But no matter how many times he asked, his body and brain reacted with 'threat'.

Mùchén left his room and went out to his mum. He told her that he was worried something terrible would happen at camp. He believed it was safer to be with her at home. She paused and took his hand. 'When you go on camp, I am not going to die. When you return after three days of doing the things you love, I will be here.'

For Mùchén, it was like something inside his body burst open and he cried for the first time since his dad died. He wept in his mother's arms for ten minutes. That night, he slept deeply. When he woke, he felt lighter. He once again asked himself: is going on camp a threat, challenge or opportunity? This time, he could say with certainty that it was a challenge. He had to challenge his fear that something bad would happen while he was away.

Mùchén went to camp! His body was a bundle of nerves as he said goodbye to his mother. But she reassured him he was doing something scary safe, not scary dangerous. That became his positive affirmation for the whole camp: 'This is scary safe'. And he had the time of his life! Mùchén returned and his mum was there waiting for him, arms stretched open, brimming with pride for her brave son.

Listen to Grow Your Mind podcast episodes:
Threat, Challenge or Opportunity
99 times (Song)

Also, head to our Grow Your Mind website, click on the *How to be a Good Enough Kid* page and get a free copy of the activities

And to practise some of the ideas from this chapter, check out the following two pages.

WHAT THINGS MAKE YOU NERVOUS?

Read the list and work out if it's a threat, challenge or opportunity:

Public speaking

Swimming with a great white shark

Standing up to a friend

Walking alone down a dark alley at night

Asking to join in a game

Smiling at someone

Running in the cross-country carnival

Making a mistake

Letting someone new sit with you at lunch

Sticking a fork into a toaster

Going on a holiday camp without knowing anyone

THREAT	CHALLENGE	OPPORTUNITY

CHAPTER 7: HOW TO BE RESILIENT

(READ THIS OUT LOUD USING YOUR BEST ANIMAL VOICES)

NOOOOOOOOOOOOOOOO MY BABIES!
YOU SAID YOU'D PROTECT THEM!
I'M SORRY, I CAN'T SEE TOO WELL
COME ON, IT'S NOT THAT BAD
THINK POSITIVE
NOT HELPFUL
ONWARDS AND UPWARDS MY FRIEND. SING IT WITH ME ...
STOP IT OR I'LL CALL THE SHARK BACK FOR SEA URCHIN DESSERT
WHAT DOESN'T KILL YOU MAKES YOU STRONGER ...
HERE SHARKY SHARKY

HOW TO BE RESILIENT

(WHEN YOU DON'T WANT TO BE)

Relax. You aren't going to be eaten for telling a sad person to cheer up. Think of the sea urchin's fate as a cautionary tale. We've all heard about resilience. I've never met your parents, but I can say with confidence that they want you to be resilient. Your teachers do too. What about you? Do you want to be resilient? Or do you want to scream at me because, actually, you want to be sad, mad, outraged, sulky, frustrated, beyond annoyed and disappointed? What if I told you that you can be both? People tend to think that resilience is built by statements like:

- Onwards and upwards
- Time to toughen up
- Think about the children starving in Africa
- Positive thoughts – tomorrow is a new day

All these statements are wrong.com. So, what IS resilience? What does it even mean? Resilience is your ability to cope with life when sadness, setbacks, disappointments and rejections happen. If you deny what you're feeling, you're not being resilient. If you don't get help when you need it, you're not being resilient. And if you pretend you don't care, you're not being resilient.

Resilience is like a petrol tank or batteries; it's normal to be high or low in charge or fuel at different times. The trick is to keep topping up your life with resilience-building activities so when things go south in life – you miss out on something, you break an arm, you lose a loved one or you suffer a rejection – you aren't running on an empty tank. When your resilience tank is full, you'll feel all the big and uncomfortable feelings and you'll be able to cope. If you're on 'empty', you might give up on someone or something that you love. Maybe you won't let yourself be close to others. Perhaps you won't try something just in case you fail. You might be super unkind to those close to you, or you might lose all your confidence.

Here's the thing, when things don't go your way, resilience is the last thing on your mind. In fact, most people would rather poke their eyeballs with a chopstick than be resilient. But this is usually because they've heard some terrible myths about resilience:

MYTH #1 Resilience is about being tough, pretending everything is fine and burying your true feelings. No way. In fact, acting like this will erode your capacity to be resilient. It's unhealthy for your mental wellbeing. Let's say you miss out on getting a part in the musical at school. You worked hard for it and you feel disappointed. Talking about it with people you trust and letting them know how you feel will take some of the sting out of it. Journalling about it can help as well.

MYTH #2 Resilience is about getting 'over' the sadness and seeing the positive. Again, a big fat 'no' to this. Resilience is about coping. It's not about getting over stuff. It's not about forcing yourself to think something awful is actually something positive. For example, your beloved cat or dog might die. You don't have to get over it and think positive. It's super sad. It's not time for positive thoughts; it's time to feel all the feels, surround yourself with kind people and be gentle on yourself.

MYTH #3 Resilience is something you do on your own. This could not be further from the truth. You can't be resilient on your own, you need good people around you. Other people matter. A LOT. We need healthy friendships, adults we can trust and people we admire and can turn to. We need to feel we have someone who cares about us. We do not 'do' resilience alone. Having one trusted person in your life to share your problems, worries or challenges with will help you be resilient.

YOUR ANIMAL HELPERS FOR THIS CHAPTER

OCTOPUS & ELEPHANT

Now that we've busted these common myths, let's revisit our definition of resilience. Resilience is your ability to cope with life when sadness, setbacks, disappointments and rejections happen. Resilience comes from having a full tank of sleep, gratitude, positive emotions, good people and an awareness that everyone goes through tough times. Resilience is about emotional regulation. You let yourself feel all the feelings, especially the big and uncomfortable ones, and you use the tools you've learned in this book to calm down, to keep trying and to stay curious. Resilience is knowing that bad times do not last.

There are strategies you can practise to help you feel resilient. Try them out during a visit from sadness, setbacks, rejections and disappointments.

STRATEGY 1: BE A GLIMMER SEEKER

As you go about your day, take note of the good things. Nice parents? A lovely friend? Delicious snack at break time? Great art class? Gorgeous dog? There are good things in life, even on the most miserable day. You could start a practice of writing down three good things about your day, maybe in a gratitude journal at night.

Or you could notice 'glimmers'. Glimmers are small moments that help us feel calm, peaceful and joyful. Our brain tends to look for the bad, so priming it to look for glimmers is super important. They are micro moments of goodness that help your body feel less stressed out and more able to cope. Examples might include:

Patting an animal

Being outside in a beautiful place

The smell of freshly baked bread

Scented stationery

Humming or singing

Listening to music

Wrapping a soft blanket around your body

When life throws you lemons it can be hard, if not impossible, to make lemonade*. But with glimmers and an awareness of good things, you are making room on the sofa of life for the sadness AND the good. Your Elephant can help you remember to look for the good and, at the end of the day, recall those micro moments.

*This is from the saying, 'When life gives you lemons, make lemonade'. Please know - you don't have to make a positive out of every negative. Some things suck. Some things are utterly horrible. If you want to make lemonade, knock yourself out. Otherwise, stick with the lemons. It's okay to be sad.

STRATEGY 2: WE ALL GET TO SUFFER

Sounds a bit brutal, no? But one of the biggest reasons we struggle to be resilient is that we believe things should always go our way. They don't and they won't. It's the same for everyone. Part of the deal of being alive is that you will suffer. You will fail. You will stuff up. You will lose loved ones.

And it's NOT about saying, 'Oh well, it happens to everyone, who cares about my beloved chicken, Black Betty, who just got run over by the neighbour' (true story). Instead, it's about feeling and expressing your sadness without thinking you're the only one who has ever experienced loss. Humanity is full of stories of significant sadness. People get through hard times. And there's strength in remembering this, so call on your Elephant to help you do just that.

STRATEGY 3: DO THE THINGS YOU LOVE

We all get busy. You may have homework, guitar lessons, swim squad, touch footy, art club or chores. And maybe the busy things are things you love – that's brilliant! But if they're not, make sure you carve out time for the things that bring you joy.

Perhaps you love lying on the grass and looking at the clouds or reading your book or making up stories or gardening or painting rocks. Whatever it is, make time for it. Doing something you love every day is just as important as eating your veggies and popping on a hat before going out in the sunshine. When we top up our joy tank, the next time we get hit by something awful, uncomfortable or heart wrenching, we are resilient enough to cope with it. When you feel joy, you may feel like you have a spring in your step. Life feels bright and light. You have an abundance of energy.

When we feel joyful, we're more likely to solve conflict. Author and mindfulness expert, Deepak Chopra, said our capacity to feel joy might be one of the cures for a more peaceful and safer world. Who would've thought that riding your bike or jumping in the ocean might help the planet?

POSITIVE EMOTIONS

These are feelings that feel so good. You've already met gratitude. Here are a few more I'd like to introduce you to:

CURIOSITY

Curiosity is feeling ready to explore, to be open, to take in new ideas and learn more. When you feel curious, you're less likely to hate or fear something. For example, 'I wonder what this meal will taste like?' vs 'This looks disgusting, I'm not eating it.'

LOVE

Love is caring deeply for a person, pet, food or an experience. You are safe. For example, your cat sits on the end of your bed, and you immediately feel more relaxed.

AWE

When you witness something truly incredible or beautiful, you might be feeling awe. Awe can stop you in your tracks and remind you of how small you are! For example, you step outside and the sky has turned pink, purple and orange. The colours are so outrageously bright that it looks like someone has coloured them in.

PLAYFUL

When you feel playful, you are safe and have the urge to laugh. You want to be with others and spend time laughing with them. For example, you run outside to play hide and seek or wink murder or wrestling.

STRATEGY 4: CHALLENGE UNHELPFUL, PESKY AND SELF-LIMITING THOUGHTS

Thoughts are not facts. Not all thoughts are helpful. Particularly when it comes to being resilient. For example, it doesn't help us if we're facing a problem, and all we can think is: 'It's hopeless.' A helpful thought might sound something like: 'Wow, this is hard, I can do hard things.' Thoughts are the words we say to ourselves without speaking out loud. We have many thoughts each hour of the day. In fact, one study suggests we have around 60,000 thoughts per day and 90% of these are repetitive. Jeepers.

Thoughts are private. Other people don't know what we're thinking unless we tell them. People can also have different thoughts about the same thing.

At Grow Your Mind, we talk about shark thoughts and dolphin thoughts. As we have said MANY times before, we absolutely love sharks in real life, they're super important for the ecosystem*.

We use the analogy of sharks because sharks like to bite things, and a shark thought is a thought that bites you. It's not helpful. For example, when something doesn't go your way – let's say the Wi-Fi is down and you miss out on playing a game you'd been really excited about – it's okay to be disappointed, but if you have a pesky shark thought that says, 'Nothing ever goes my way; I always miss out, it's so unfair', you'll soon find these thoughts aren't helping you.

*Sharks help the planet! Sharks play a crucial role in slowing climate change. Take tiger sharks in Western Australia – they make oceans more resilient to climate change by swimming around the shallow seagrass meadows, preventing marine creatures from overgrazing. This helps seagrass become denser and more abundant. And get this? Do you know what captures carbon from the atmosphere 35 times faster than tropical rainforests? Yes, that's right – seagrass!

What about dolphin thoughts? Dolphins have been known to help people in danger at sea. Seeing a dolphin shoot through the air can help you out of a bad mood; it lifts your spirits. Dolphin thoughts do the same. They help you out. Let's go back to the Wi-Fi dropping out situation. Is there a dolphin way of looking at this? It might sound like this: 'That's so disappointing, but I guess everyone misses out sometimes.' This is a key part of being resilient: working out if a thought or an action is helping or harming you and choosing to zoom in on the helpful thought instead.

HOW TO HAVE DOLPHIN THOUGHTS

1. NOTICE WHEN YOU'RE HAVING A SHARK THOUGHT (REMEMBER IT'S OKAY TO FEEL SAD, BUT IF YOU'RE HAVING A THOUGHT THAT ISN'T HELPFUL, JUST NOTICE IT).

2. ASK: 'IS THERE A MORE HELPFUL WAY TO LOOK AT THIS?'

Maybe you feel uncomfortable in the clothes you're wearing, and you start thinking horrible things about your body. Pause and ask: 'Is there a more helpful way to look at this?' You might think, 'My body helps me do the things I love – I should treat it with love'. Perhaps you get a B instead of an A in maths. Rather than thinking you're a failure, you might think, 'I worked hard and did well; now I know what areas I need extra help with.'

Quick warning – when something truly bad happens it is NOT the time for dolphin thinking. Let yourself feel all the feels. No need for dolphin thoughts straight away.

WHAT TO DO ABOUT PERSISTENT SHARK THOUGHTS

Here's a trick: take the power away from the shark thought by giving it a name. For example, you might think 'I am not enough.' Respond to that thought with, 'Shhh, Frank!' or 'Shhh, Gertrude!' Insert any name you like. You can challenge shark thoughts by creating resilient thoughts. Think of a shark thought you currently have, now complete these sentences:

That thought is not true because ...
Another way of thinking about this is ...
The most likely outcome is ...

When you challenge pesky, self-limiting thoughts, you're also building skills in 'positive reappraisal'. Sounds fancy, but it's not *that* fancy. You might recall that our brains create stories about events and situations to make sense of things. Our brains will often jump to the worst conclusions. If we use positive reappraisal, we can reinterpret events or situations in a more positive manner. But we need our Sensitive Octopus and our Elephant to combine powers and help us. Our Elephant will help us remember that we create stories, and that thoughts are not facts. Our Sensitive Octopus will help us look at this story and come to a more generous assumption about other people's behaviour.

Reminder - none of these steps will help you feel resilient if you're alone. You need good people in your life to be and feel resilient. Channel your Sensitive Octopus to help you make and keep fantastic friends.

Practise challenging unhelpful thoughts using this positive reappraisal guide:

CHALLENGE UNHELPFUL THOUGHTS BY IDENTIFYING THEM AS A SHARK THOUGHT

TELL YOURSELF, THE STORY I'M TELLING MYSELF IS ... E.G. THE STORY I'M TELLING MYSELF IS THAT YOU DON'T LIKE ME ANYMORE

CREATE THE START OF A RESILIENT DOLPHIN THOUGHT ... E.G. THAT THOUGHT ISN'T TRUE BECAUSE ...

REWRITE THE STORY OF WHAT HAPPENED. ASK YOURSELF, WHAT IS THE MOST GENEROUS ASSUMPTION I COULD MAKE RIGHT NOW?

Practise using the guide with the following three scenarios:

1. YOUR FRIEND SAYS HE CANNOT HANG OUT ON THE WEEKEND, BUT YOU RIDE PAST HIS PLACE ON SATURDAY AND HE'S KICKING A FOOTY WITH THREE OF YOUR MATES.

2. YOUR FRIEND HAS TWO CLOSE FRIENDS FOR A SLEEPOVER AND DOESN'T INVITE YOU.

3. YOUR FRIEND REMOVES YOU FROM A GROUP CHAT YOU'VE BEEN PART OF FOR A YEAR. THE NEXT DAY HE SAYS IT WAS AN ACCIDENT AND ADDS YOU BACK IN.

You've been practising the steps to being resilient. Your tank is full. But then something terrible happens to you. You need to talk about it. If you can't talk to a friend or a trusted adult and you live in Australia, try calling the KidsHelp line on 1800 551 800. Is there a similar service in your country? Do you have access to a school counsellor? Secrets should never be kept when bad things happen. It's important to tell someone. You are not alone. We cannot be or feel resilient without other people. Get your Elephant to help you write a list of the people you can trust, ask your Sensitive Octopus to select the most trustworthy of the lot. If the bad thing is super disappointing (but not terrible) and you don't feel resilient, you can try this ...

FOCUS ON WHAT YOU CAN CONTROL

Working out what we can and can't control is super helpful. You can do it for big and small problems. Find a piece of paper and draw a circle on the page. In the middle of the circle, write down all the things you can control about a situation. On the outside of the circle, write down all the things you cannot control. Make a mental note to let go of the things you can't control, because there is nothing you can do about it. Focus on what you can control. Take action.

THINGS I CAN'T CONTROL

Missing out

The weather

How long things might take

If someone likes me or not

THINGS I CAN CONTROL

Looking for glimmers
Moving my body
Assuming people are doing the best they can
How kind I am to myself and others
Challenging unhelpful thoughts

Now I want to introduce one of the researchers whose work has inspired this chapter: Dr Lucy Hone. Dr Hone is a legend and a leader in the field of resilient grieving. Her story is heartbreaking. She lost her best friend as well as her own gorgeous 12-year-old daughter in a car accident. Suddenly, Dr Hone had to apply her research to her real life; resilience was life-saving and life-affirming for herself and her loved ones.

Dr Hone says people tend to think resilience is about being tough and calm all the time. But, in fact, it's not. Our favourite quote from Dr Hone is this one: 'Resilience is not pretty'. We love it. It gives us permission to cry, to feel all the feels AND to keep going. That's the goal, good enough kid. We want you to participate in life, no matter what mud gets thrown at you, and to never forget how loved you are.

BRAIN BREAK:

What animal am I?

I evolved over 420 million years ago. That means I am 200 million years older than dinosaurs. My skeleton is cartilage (the same thing your nose and ears are made of).

Share these facts tonight at dinner (and distract your parents from asking you to clear the table):

Saltwater crocodiles used to eat dinosaurs.

The Goliath birdeater spider spans the width of a dinner plate and can grow back lost limbs.

SHINE THE SPOTLIGHT ON ...

SAM BLOOM:

WORLD PARA SURFING CHAMPION, AUTHOR + MAGPIE WHISPERER

"Unlike most people, I don't wake wondering if my day is going to be good or bad. It is always going to be bad unless I actively do something to make it good. And nothing feels as good as helping others."

Research Challenge: Find out what you can about Sam's story. Why do you think we have spotlighted her in this chapter?

THE DAY A PUDDLE GOT THE BETTER OF ONDINE

It had been raining heavily that morning, but the sun came out and Ondine was off to play AFL. At the beginning of the second quarter, Ondine's team was down two points with no subs. Tensions were high. She'd made some great tackles, passes and kicks. But then, disaster struck! Ondine's foot got lodged in a mud puddle. She turned her body, and launched herself into a tackle, but her leg didn't follow. There was a loud snapping sound, and the pain that followed was instantly unbearable. Ondine's lower leg had broken in two places. She was taken to the hospital and the doctors told her she would need to be in a wheelchair for at least four months. She would need help to use the bathroom, and she would have to manage her pain with painkillers and stay in bed. They kept her in the hospital for five days. She went from feeling scared, to furious, to super courageous, to amused and back again. Most of all, Ondine hated feeling vulnerable. She did not like relying on others. This was going to be hard.

Her parents tried to remind her that lots of people had been through something similar and she would get through it. Ondine did NOT want to think about this. In fact, any mention of this would result in eye-rolling, sighing, the occasional 

and a deathly silence. The pain put her in a dark mood. She said mean things and yelled out of frustration. You see, Ondine was a bright, loving kid who liked order and routine; she relied on two things to feel calm and safe: exercise and being able to bathe. Both were taken away from her.

Despite feeling down and grumpy about all the things she could no longer do, Ondine discovered there were still things she loved and could do. She adored going around Centennial Park in her wheelchair, turning her beloved dog into a sled dog. Ondine realised that focusing on things she could do brought her joy and made her feel better.

When the time came for Ondine to return to school, she felt anxious about how she would manage. Her classroom was up two flights of stairs. What about break time? Everyone liked being active, what would she do?

To her surprise, her friends and classmates were kinder than she imagined. They carried her school bag, played inside games and the class moved to a different room to make it more accessible for her.

After what felt like an eternity, Ondine was able to walk again! She still had to do rehab twice a week to rebuild her strength. Ondine set herself a goal during her recovery: she wanted to hike the Three Capes in Tasmania and play AFL again. Ondine knew she could do hard things with good people around her. And guess what? She did both. Legend.

Listen to Grow Your Mind podcast episodes:
You Can't Grow It Alone
Love Without A Home
Resilience (Song)

Try this the next time you face a setback: draw a circle. Write down all the things that are beyond your control outside of the circle, then write down the things you can control inside the circle.

Complete a positive emotions planner. Jump onto our website to download the template.

CHAPTER 8: HOW TO BE OKAY WITH BEING AVERAGE

(READ THIS OUT LOUD USING YOUR BEST ANIMAL VOICES)

WELL, I'M TIRED OF NEVER WINNING!
I'M THE WORST - THEY CALL ME THE BIN CHICKEN
WELL NOT ALL BIRDS CAN LIVE TO 28
AND LOOK HOW SLENDER AND CURVED YOUR BILL IS
I'D RATHER A SPOONY ONE LIKE THE ROSEATE SPOONBILL
IBIS, ALL THE OTHER BEAKS ARE TAKEN! BE YOU. BE PROUD.
YOU EAT BUGS THAT DESTROY GARDENS
YOU FIGHT LOCUST PLAGUES FOR FARMERS!
YOUR HOME WAS DESTROYED BUT YOU ADAPTED TO BE A BIN CHICKEN
PLUS, YOU ALWAYS SHARE YOUR WORMS WITH ME
THAT'S TRUE, I'M QUITE GOOD AT SHARING
YOU'RE A SURVIVOR
FOCUS ON THAT

HOW TO BE OKAY WITH BEING AVERAGE

Have you, like our ibis friend, ever felt frustrated that you're not the best? Maybe you never get awards in assembly unless it's for wearing your uniform, which just feels humiliating. It's like they're saying, 'Here's a certificate for putting your clothes on.' Please. Or perhaps you never get voted class captain or win races. It's time to reclaim the power of average people.

WHY IS BEING AVERAGE A GOOD THING?

Practically speaking, we can't all be the best. Usually there's only one winner, one first place, one medal for best and fairest. Unless you're playing the version of pass the parcel where everyone wins a prize (Tina, my dear friend and Grow Your Mind co-founder, has a SERIOUS issue with this). If you're playing the Tina-preferred, high-stakes, pass-the-parcel rules then, good enough reader, you need to get better at being average.

WINNING ISN'T WHAT LIVING A GOOD LIFE IS ABOUT

Poor mental health is a massive issue for humans. There are varied and complex explanations for this, but I don't think the pressure to be extraordinary helps. Have you ever longed to be perfect at something? (I hope you crossed out that word.) Maybe it's a secret wish to have flawless skin, abs of steel, unbelievable smarts or a singing voice that inspires people to rise to their feet in admiration?

I know it's hard to believe, but a good life involves none of these. Instead, it's about being surrounded by good people you can rely on, being a kind person, having purpose and doing things you love. You won't win a place for these things, but you will feel it in your body and heart.

JUST BE HERE

If you're constantly looking over your shoulder, comparing yourself with others, longing to be different or better you miss the gift of this exquisite moment in time, happening right now! You're alive today. So BE alive. Get your Sifting Sooty to help you focus on the here and now. Now, I know being told to 'just be here' and 'winning isn't everything' is not going to soothe the sting of disappointment. It hurts. So, this chapter is dedicated to helping you deal with those disappointments. Plus, I'll show you a few ways to pull yourself out of a Comparison Poop Storm. Oh, and the other poop storm I'm hoping to steer you out of is the Perfectionist Poop Storm. Believe me, it's the stinkiest storm you can find yourself in.

This chapter isn't about denying the excitement of being a champion. Full disclaimer – I love to win. In fact, we all love to win. I particularly enjoy the satisfaction of winning when someone is being a total punish. Boast excessively about your skills or knock another person down, and I will destroy you in backyard cricket with every fibre of my being! This chapter isn't about shaming winning. It's just to say, hey – don't make it all about winning because you'll end up losing in the game of living a good life.

And if you're someone who often wins, this chapter is still for you because even if you're winning today, you will lose one day. The fact is, we ALL need a mindset shift when it comes to the topic of winning. And our Sifting Sooty can help us refocus and make this shift.

SIFTING SOOTY

So, what are the steps to really rocking your inner average? Here are my top three:

DEVELOP A GROWTH MINDSET

A growth mindset* means you see mistakes as a learning opportunity; you believe your intelligence can grow. To have a growth mindset, you need supportive people around you. So, good enough kid, if you're reading this and your friends, parents or teachers shame you for making mistakes, I understand. It's HARD, if not impossible, to have a growth mindset. However, I want you to hold onto this: mistakes and challenges are the key to lifelong learning. Learning new things can be tricky, but it's incredibly healthy for your brain and mental health.

***Mindset**

A set of beliefs you have about yourself. These beliefs shape how you behave and determine your outlook on life.

Let's take a look at what's happening in your brain when you're learning. Do you remember that fancy term, 'neuroplasticity', from Chapter 2? Our brains can change and grow. When you learn new things, your brain uses neurotransmitters to send messages from one neuron to another, again and again. Your brain will start to create pathways between the neurons, and you'll become more confident and better at the thing you're learning.

I'm not going to pretend to be an expert in neuroscience (that would be ridiculous and dangerous), but I do believe that knowing a bit about the brain and how we learn can help us develop a growth mindset. You have neurons in your brain. They are tiny brain cells which receive and send information. You have roughly 100 billion of them. They look a bit like this:

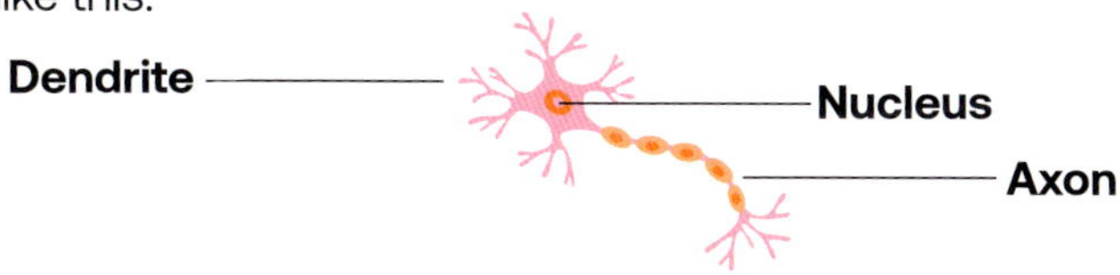

Lots of people think of neurons as a tree. If you look at the things called 'dendrites' in the image, they look like branches of a tree, do they not? And get this, when we learn new things, the dendrites grow higher and higher, and new dendrites sprout out of the existing ones. Look closely at the next image. Do you see how the two 'branches' are almost touching, but there's still a gap between them?

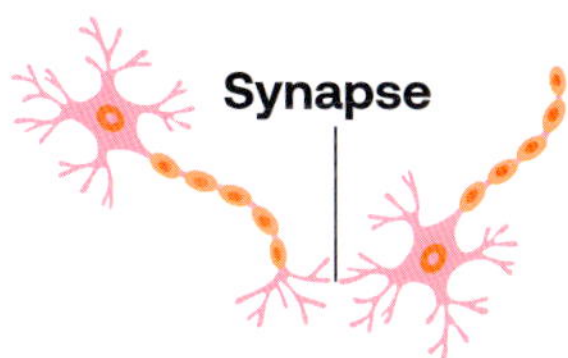

That gap is called a 'synapse'. And this is where the trusty neurotransmitters come into play. They are chemical messengers. They send Information between neurons by crossing the synapse.

New dendrites take time and a lot of practice to grow – which means it can take some time for us to learn things. Learning new things can be a frustrating process. This is where a growth mindset helps. A growth mindset is about having faith that you will and can improve. It reminds us that we can do hard things, make mistakes and keep trying.

A growth mindset is all about the process, not the outcome. Let's say you're trying to land an ollie in skateboarding. You practise, but you can't do it yet, so you practise again and again and again. And you still can't do it. It's so tempting to give up. But if you know that learning something new is hard, if you have supportive people around you and if you feel safe to keep trying, your dendrites will start doing their thing.

A growth mindset helps you to really rock your inner average by practising something purely for the love of it – or for the love of dendrite growth!

BE YOURSELF

You have full permission to rock your inner weird AND rejoice in all your imperfections. The first question we should ask a potential new friend is: 'So, what's weird about you?' Actually, don't take my advice on that one. Might be a tad strange. My point is: start noticing who you are, what you love, what frustrates and motivates you and what music you like. Get your Sifting Sooty to focus on that.

There was once a famous philosopher* called Socrates. He lived in Athens a looonnng time ago (469 BC – 399 BC). Socrates believed the key to a good life was knowing who you are: 'self-knowledge'. It's important to know who you are because, without self-knowledge, you might make choices that aren't true to you.

***Philosopher**

People who study philosophy (which means love of wisdom). Philosophy is the study of some of life's big questions. For example, what is the meaning of life? Are human beings basically good or evil? Does free will exist? Philosophers observe the world, experiment and think.

Picture this: you're the best at swimming in your year and you dominate every carnival. Your coaches want you to swim four mornings a week, but you don't like swimming that much. You say 'no', and you sleep in or spend the mornings riding your bike instead. You know yourself, so you choose not to spend your precious childhood doing something you don't enjoy just because you might win. Instead, you spend it living your good life.

Your Sifting Sooty can help you work out what your good life is by asking: 'What do I love? When do I feel at my best?'

CONDUCT AN INTERVIEW WITH YOURSELF

Here's a chance to get to know yourself better. You are the interviewer AND the interviewee. Grab some paper and record your answers:

Who are you when no one is looking?
What do you love?
What matters to you?
How do you live your best life?

SELF-IDENTITY

What matters to you? What do you love to do? What makes you, you? This is what identity means (the qualities, characteristics or beliefs that make a person who they are). Grab a piece of paper and draw the outline of a head and neck. Fill the face with things you love and that matter to you. It could be drawings, images, symbols – anything that represents your self-identify.

KNOW AND GROW A STRENGTH TODAY!

KNOW YOUR CHARACTER STRENGTHS AND USE THEM

We all have character strengths. They are the positive qualities that show up in our thoughts, feelings and actions. When you know your best ones, you can use them to overcome challenges, get better at things and thrive.

There are no prizes for character strengths. No one can be the winner of perseverance or love or kindness. There is no first place. You simply possess these strengths and can use them to benefit yourself and others.

Did you know you're also growing more character strengths? For example, I'm pretty strong at gratitude; I can easily see the good things in my life. But I'm still growing patience. I struggle when things take longer than I thought they would. I'm okay sitting in traffic, but I'm not okay when my children can't find their school shoes and the bus is coming. I sigh loudly and stomp. But I'm growing patience and I have rockstar times when I might say things like, 'Whoa, I'm really struggling to be patient. I feel like having an adult tantrum!' If I name the strength I'm trying to use, it helps me (and my Sifting Sooty) focus on what I should be doing.

WHAT ARE YOUR TOP FOUR-CHARACTER STRENGTHS?

Before you answer, you need to give evidence of the strength. I'll start! One of my strengths is gratitude. The evidence? I focus on what I do have, not what I don't have. I'm healthy, I love my job, I adore my family and I rarely feel as though my life would be better if I had more.

Finding evidence of our strengths is important. Being told you're great at everything isn't as powerful as seeing the proof for yourself. Look at the character strengths in the balloon on page 191 – do any of them jump out at you?

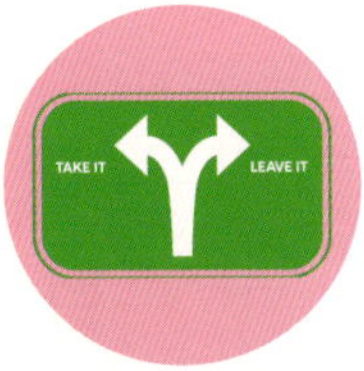

BE A STRENGTH SPOTTER

I'm guessing you're currently reading a book other than this one. What strengths does the character in your book possess? Maybe you're reading the *Harry Potter* series? If you had to identify Harry's strength, what would it be? What about Moana? Or Puss in Boots? Still stuck? What about your friends and family? Can you name their strengths?

Knowing and using your character strengths isn't about winning or being the best. It's about being the best version of you. You might not be picked for the team or for a part in the school play. Maybe you don't get a good grade – it's okay, you're still YOU with your unique character strengths. And being average and using your character strengths for good actually makes you a legend of a human being.

It still feels rubbish to miss out on something you care a lot about. Here's some extra tips for finding your way out of a Comparison Poop Storm and a Perfectionist Poop Storm.

Remember mental fitness? Being mentally fit can really help you overcome the ouch-y-ness of disappointments. 'Cool,' you say. 'Sign me up to the best mental fitness gym in town, I'm ready to lift some brainy weights.' It's not quite like that. I'm not saying your brain is a muscle that can be worked out (it's an organ not a muscle). But we can, however, improve our mental health with the right training.

If you practise these things and maintain some level of mental fitness, you can feel all the feels while still being able to participate in life.

Mental fitness training not only helps you feel okay with being average, it helps you celebrate it. If you really want to rock your inner average and let your weird and imperfect ways shine, mental fitness will help you ride the waves of life.

Okay, almost out of the poop storm, what else have I got?

GROW AN ABUNDANCE MINDSET

An abundance mindset is when you believe the world is full of enough resources and time for you to accomplish your goals. If you're not winning or being recognised, you still believe you can live a good life and do the things you want. A scarcity mindset is the opposite. You're fixated on what you're missing out on, what you don't have and what you didn't win.

Picture this – someone gets an award. An abundance mindset might sound like, 'Good for them! I have other things in my life and plenty of time to achieve my goals.' (Said NO kid ever.) Whereas a scarcity mindset might sound like, 'That's so unfair. I never win, I'm a loser.' (Said most kids.)

HOW DO YOU GET AN ABUNDANCE MINDSET?

You need your trusty helper, the Sifting Sooty, to come to the abundance mindset party. Remember, the questions you ask and what you focus on will shape your beliefs. If we ask ourselves unhelpful questions ('Why do I suck?') and we focus on the negative ('Here are all the reasons I suck'), then we won't look for the positives. We will believe that we actually do suck. This is where that pesky G word – gratitude – comes back! If you never win or things don't go your way, you can keep things in perspective by focusing on all that you do have and all that you are.

You can apply gratitude to any part of your life. Consider body gratitude, where you focus on what your body can do, and refrain from comparing it with how others look or what they can do.

ONE FINAL TIP FOR NAVIGATING OUT OF THE POOP STORMS

Have you ever heard of the saying: **a blessing in disguise?** What do you think it means? Here's an example of a blessing in disguise: you miss out on being selected for the top footy team, but you end up in a team with friendly kids and less pressure. In fact, the kids in the top team are always fighting and being unkind. Some of the top team players drop out; they lose their love for the game. Meanwhile, you're having the time of your life. Not making the best team was a blessing in disguise. It's just a good reminder that sometimes failing or missing out can end up being a better thing than getting what you want.

BRAIN BREAK:

What animal am I?
I survive on a diet of highly toxic eucalyptus leaves, but my digestive system is equipped with a special bacterium to digest these otherwise deadly greens. I am outrageously cute, but I can also be ruthless.

Share this fact with someone:
When octopus mammas are expecting babies, they get hungry and eat their own arms.

SHINE THE SPOTLIGHT ON ...

HARRY GARSIDE:

BOXER, PLUMBER + BALLET DANCER

An Olympic boxer, really? In a chapter about celebrating being average? Yes, yes, I know, Harry has won championships and a bronze medal at the Olympics. But he is the epitome of someone who has a growth mindset, and he found his self-worth outside of winning. But hey, I'm doing the work for you!

> *"We all hate shooting for the stars and falling on our face. But I had this realisation that I went on this two-decade journey to try and get that gold medal and yes, I didn't get that gold medal, but I've become my own friend in that journey."*

Research Challenge: Find out about Harry's take on being knocked out of the first round at the Olympic Games in Paris 2024.

DEALING WITH DISAPPOINTMENT – THE STORY OF VIOLET B

Violet had a goal. Ever since kindergarten she wanted to be music captain more than anything. She worked hard for it. She joined multiple music groups, and she sang and played the guitar all the time. She was sure she'd get the role because no one else in her grade seemed interested. Plus, she'd been at the school since kindergarten – surely that meant she deserved it more than people who came later?

One day, a new girl arrived. Her name was Zoe. Like Violet, she was hard-working and passionate about music. Voting day came around, and everyone cast their vote for the new school representatives. One week later, the students filed into the assembly hall, waiting to hear the results. Violet had prepared her acceptance speech and her handshake. The principal stepped up to the microphone to announce the successful candidates. 'Your new music captain will be,' she began, then glanced down at her notes. 'Zoe.'

Ouch. It hurt.

Violet cried for days and days. It wasn't fair! She couldn't believe she hadn't been chosen. She felt like a failure. Violet didn't know how to move on from her sadness and her anger. Every time she passed Zoe she looked down. She lashed out at her family and other friends, who had no idea why they were receiving such bitter treatment from her. Violet felt on edge; she was not sure how to calm down. Eventually, she turned to the one thing that always brought her joy: she played her guitar.

She strummed and hummed some Tracy Chapman, realising that missing out on being music captain didn't change her love of music. She would always love music. She also realised that missing out on music captain didn't mean she hadn't tried her hardest or that Zoe was less deserving. It's just the way things had worked out.

Violet started to say a positive affirmation to herself every night. She told herself: 'I'm enough, I'm unique and I don't need to change.' Over time, these affirmations helped build her confidence back up again.

These days, Violet still plays and loves her guitar. She believes she will for the rest of her life. Violet shared with us that 'Awards are nice, but doing something because you love it is an even better reward.'

Listen to Grow Your Mind podcast episodes:
Ouch This Hurts

Head to our website, click on the *How to be a Good Enough Kid* page and get a free copy of the activities.

Think about a time you were disappointed about something. Where does it fit on the Guard Dog Problem Scale?

Remember, it's okay to feel whatever you want to feel. Just focus on what you need from your Guard Dog to survive.

CHAPTER 9: HOW TO BE THE BOSS OF YOUR DEVICE

(READ THIS OUT LOUD USING YOUR BEST ANIMAL VOICES)

OH, IT'S OK, IT'S HERE
I MISSED YOU
WHEN WAS THE LAST TIME YOU WENT OUTSIDE?
UMMMMMMMMMMM YESTERDAY? NO, THE DAY BEFORE.
WHEN WAS THE LAST TIME YOU MOVED YOUR BODY?
MY PAWS AND TAIL MOVE A LOT
LIGHTEN UP! TECHNOLOGY IS INCREDIBLE!
YEAH, IT IS
BUT YOU'VE TURNED INTO A SCREENAGER
OH GOSH, IS THAT A SICKNESS? WHAT'S THE CURE?
REPLACE SCREEN TIME WITH GREEN TIME
BRILLIANT. I LOVE GREEN SCREEN.

HOW TO BE THE BOSS OF YOUR DEVICE

Full disclaimer: my phone is currently hidden in a drawer in a different room. It's not because I hate my phone. It's because despite my best intentions, I'm obsessed with it.

I'm so easily drawn to my phone; every time a message pops up, I look at it. Every time I feel a little restless, I find myself picking it up. I read the news or mindlessly scroll sweet wombat videos, which lead me to octopus clips, and then I'm down a rabbit hole of saving our seas from plastic and discovering why eating sustainable fish is the only way forward and, hang on, is that Beyoncé picking up plastic rubbish while scuba diving in the Maldives? And then I glance at the time and realise I've spent an hour on my phone. A whole hour! I just wanted to see what was happening in today's news, and I've been sucked into a vortex. And here lies the problem. We are not the boss of our devices; they are the boss of us. Unless, my technology-addicted friend, we take back control! Maybe you're not addicted yet, but if you think you can escape the YouTube algorithm, which suggests videos after you've been innocently perfecting your maths with Eddie Woo, think again. Now you too are down the rabbit hole of fishing rods, Minecraft tips and survival skills ...

You'll be relieved to hear me say: I love technology. I love the internet. Thanks to technology, I can have a proper connection with my super interesting and intelligent friend who is non-verbal. She is a talented writer, has cerebral palsy, and when we were younger it was harder to communicate. But these days we text, we share posts on social media and we email. I feel like I really know her, and technology gives her a platform to feel seen and heard.

You may also be relieved to hear that I'm not telling you to stop gaming. Some video games help you with things like working memory and impulse control*. And, of course, they're super fun. I will be telling you to go outside, to seek awe and look for glimmers (like drinking a delicious hot chocolate, petting your dog or soaking in a warm bath). I want you to move your body, to connect with people and to set some very strong boundaries, but more on that in a moment.

*WORKING MEMORY + IMPULSE CONTROL

Working memory allows us to hold information in our mind for a short period of time while we're doing other activities. For example, you can memorise a phone number while looking for a pen to write it down. Or you can remember the instruction your teacher has given you while you're finishing up something else. Working memory helps you do these things!

Impulse control is your ability to have willpower or command over your actions or emotions. Impulse control is super tricky, especially for you legendary, good enough kids. Your Guard Dog needs training – you're still learning which things are threats, challenges and opportunities. And your Wise Owl, in charge of good decisions, needs time to grow – the prefrontal cortex doesn't fully develop until you're 25.

YOUR ANIMAL HELPER FOR THIS CHAPTER

DIGITAL DISTRACTION

Did you know, adults can focus for about six minutes before they become digitally distracted? Do you ever feel a similar pull to your phone, iPad or some other device? Here's my vision: I want to see all of us using technology in healthy and helpful ways and not be forever missing out on the present moment. And to do that, we all need to admit we need stronger boundaries around using our devices. These can be put in place by you or your parents. Or even the government can assist in restricting access to social media. Or your dog. Or an intimidating don't-mess-with-me-cat. Take your pick.

You might ask, what's the problem with being distracted by puppy videos? Well, my puppy-loving reader, there are three BIG problems. Without boundaries on content and usage, technology can:

- Lessen our ability to be bored
- Negatively impact our mental health
- Put us at greater risk of obesity and general physical unfitness because we're not moving our bodies enough

Allow me to elaborate on the pros of being bored. Our brains were never designed to be switched on and constantly processing information. Our brains need opportunities to daydream. When we're bored, we wonder; we have the mental space to come up with creative ideas or solutions to problems. When we daydream, we get a chance to imagine and understand who we are.

Technology is not going away. It touches every aspect of our lives. So, we need to learn to live with it in healthy ways.

You and your family can look up experts in the world of digital safety. For example, if you live in Australia, the eSafety Commissioner has some fantastic resources on how to be safe online, what to do if someone is cyberbullying you, how to pick if something is fake news and loads more. And parents, if you're reading this, the eSafety Commissioner also has a space for you with tips and tricks for managing screen time and keeping everyone safe.

THE GROW YOUR MIND SCREEN TIME GUIDE

Talk about technology as a family

You and your family can work out a healthy way to use your devices. Agree on the content (make it positive stuff) and balance online and offline activities. For example, you might opt for no screens before midday or maybe you're required to move your body before you touch a device. Use your Wise Owl for this chat, it will help you weigh up the pros and cons, be flexible and predict the outcomes of decisions.

Get your DOSE of wellbeing before you turn on your device

DOSE is an acronym for neurotransmitters; you know, those helpful chemical messengers that send information between neurons, making us feel energised, upbeat, calm, loved and more. Oh yeah!

D DOPAMINE

O OXYTOCIN

S SERATONIN

E ENDORPHINS

Here are some quick ways to get your DOSE of wellbeing before you turn to technology:

- Dopamine makes you feel motivated; it brings on a sense of reward. Bring it on by popping on some music you love, making a list of what you want to get done that day and making sure you've slept well.
- Oxytocin makes you feel relaxed, loving and generous. Get it by performing an act of kindness for someone, hugging a trusted person for 20 seconds and connecting with a human in real time.
- Serotonin makes you feel happier and calmer. Get it by heading outside, putting your face to the sun (wearing a hat when the ultraviolet (UV) radiation level is high) and eating something healthy and nourishing.
- Endorphins makes you feel less pain and put you in a better mood. Get it by moving those bun buns! Exercise. Not with your fingers on a device – get outside and move your body.

Make your bedroom tech-free

Why? You need your sleep – we all do. There was once a super mean study where they took different rats and denied them either water, food or sleep. The first rats to die? Those without water. The second? Those without sleep. When we sleep, your Elephant (the hippocampus) helps you remember things you have learned during the day. If your phone starts pinging, you won't be able to sleep, and your Elephant can't do its job.

Hide your device when you don't need it

That tech thingy can feel like an extension of your arm or soul, so hide it for a bit. You don't need your device to cook - use a recipe book. You don't need it to read your textbook or when you're chatting with a sibling. Hide it, give it a kiss if you really need to, then walk away.

Good enough kids need natural sunlight every week. Yes, with your hats and sunscreen on. You need sunlight because it helps regulate your circadian rhythm*, which helps with sleep.

***Circadian rhythm**

Our body's internal clock. Circadian rhythms are the physical, mental and behavioral changes that we experience over a 24-hour cycle. Circadian rhythms play a vital role in our ability to experience refreshing, restorative sleep in one consolidated block of time.

Have a complete digital disconnection once a day

And boy, do I have some ideas! If you're panicking at the thought of being disconnected from your device, fear not – it's going to be okay.

But before I jump excitedly into my ideas for daily disconnections, I want to speak directly to you, reader. Every time you post anything online, it becomes part of your digital footprint. You ate Vegemite toast in 2025? People will be able to uncover this fascinating fact about you in 2055. It also means if you write something unkind or rude about someone online, it will be part of your digital footprint ... forever.

So, before you post that your old friend is a smelly poo whose personality is as interesting as a flea's, pause and **THINK!**

IS IT ...

T	H	I	N	K
True?	Helpful?	Important?	Necessary?	Kind?

Will you want people to read what you wrote about your friend in the future? If you take a photo of you doing something that seemed hilarious, but is actually inappropriate or truly stupid, pause before you post. It will be on the internet throughout your entire life. Even if you share a private photo of yourself with only one person, and you think that photo is just for them, it will exist throughout your entire life.

If the whole THINK acronym is NOT enough to stop you from writing something mean or sharing a dicey photo – then turn to your Wise Owl. Think how you might feel about the post in five, ten or 50 years from now. This is your digital footprint. We all have one.

USE YOUR TIME ON EARTH TO BE AN ...

Awe hunter

Someone who deliberately seeks out experiences that stop them in their tracks. This type of hunter is amazed by something which, in turn, helps their problems feel smaller.

Glimmer seeker

Someone who seeks moments of joy and peace by noticing small, daily, pleasant things.

Question asker

Someone who shows curiosity about people, places and the world.

So why aim to be an awe hunter, glimmer seeker and question asker? Because it's a surefire way to make life feel less overwhelming. It will boost positive feelings of gratitude and curiosity.

WE FEEL AWE WHEN SOMETHING AMAZES US

This could be a mountain, an outstanding music performance, a fascinating animal, a night sky jam-packed with stars, witnessing incredible kindness or learning about amazing people.

When we feel awe, cool things happen to our mental wellbeing. We feel more capable of solving problems than we first thought. This might be because awe sparks creativity. And when we think creatively, we become better problem solvers.

Awe inspires us to be more generous. During one study, half of the participants were asked to stare up at a beautiful tree while the other half were asked to stare at an ordinary building. The researchers then staged a scene where someone walked past and dropped their pens on the ground. The people who had been admiring the tree picked up more pens than those who had been looking at a building. Awe brought out their kind and helpful side.

SO HOW DO YOU BECOME AN AWE HUNTER?

Well, get your binoculars and pocketknife and be ready to drink your own blood – you are going out into the remote wilderness. You may never see another human again and when you do, you might eat them. But hey, it'll be worth it! You might feel awe and behave more generously to the next human you see (and only eat their knee).

Nah - luckily, we can feel awe right here at home. Put down that device and step outside. Grab a trusted adult and jump on a bike (or go by yourself if it's safe and you have permission). What is the sky like? How about the clouds or the trees? Head to the local park, river or ocean. Feeling awe means you must be present; you must be here – now – and not looking down at a screen.

WHY BE A GLIMMER SEEKER?

Glimmers can help calm the nervous system and return us to a regulated state, especially after we have felt stressed out or worried about something. When we seek glimmers, we feel more at ease. Things are going to be okay. Noticing glimmers is a type of gratitude practice; you're aware of something around you that brings joy, peace, love and calmness.

HOW DO YOU SEEK GLIMMERS?

You don't have to chase glimmers! Put away your device and notice and enjoy the small moments. If we're strapped to the screen all day, we don't give ourselves the opportunity to notice any potential glimmers.

BE A QUESTION ASKER

Well, be a good question asker. Don't just ask:

What's for dinner?
Can I watch TV?
Where's my iPad?

A good question asker wants to know more about people and the world. A good question asker is not just asking in the hope they might get asked a question back so they can talk about their favourite topic of conversation – themselves!

It can feel butt-clenchingly awkward and stilted to ask questions at first, so maybe start with something light-hearted:

- Dad, if you had any magic power for 24 hours, what would it be and why?
- Mum, when you were little, did you think your life would be like it is now? Why/why not?
- Sister, if you could steal something and no one would ever know you stole it, what would it be and why?
- Brother, if you could transform into an African animal, what would it be and why?

Asking questions is a great way to make friends with people. Asking questions means you're growing curiosity. When we're curious, we're less judgemental. This is an excellent thing. Why? Look at you, you incredible question asker! It's great because instead of jumping to the worst conclusions about people, we approach heated moments with curiosity. You ask questions before you form your opinions.

Good question askers listen to the answer properly. They don't look down at their device or over their shoulder at what their other friend is doing. They listen. They are present.

BRAIN BREAK:

What animal am I?

When biologists first found me (dead) they sent me to London from Australia and people thought it was a HOAX. Someone had clearly killed a duck and stuck its poor beak onto the body of another fluffy animal with strange, webbed feet. They were wrong. I'm very shy, I have a beautiful coat like an otter, webbed toes and a soft leathery bill.

Share these facts with someone:

The combined weight of the world's microbes* is around 50 times more than the combined weight of the world's animals.

Knobbed hornbills are a bird native to Indonesia. They stop snakes from eating their eggs by blocking off the entrance to their nests with their own poop.

***Microbes**

Living things so small you can only see them with a microscope. They're found in water, soil, the air and our bodies.

SHINE THE SPOTLIGHT ON ...

GINA CHICK:

ALONE AUSTRALIA WINNER, WRITER + REWILDING FACILITATOR

> *"Go and find a park and kick off your shoes and close your eyes and squish your feet into the grass and let the sun hit your face. Take a couple of deep breaths. And all of a sudden you're plugging into the battery of wild nature and allowing energy to come up through your bare feet, which is traditionally how our hunter-gatherer ancestors would spend a large part of their time walking on the Earth, with a footprint, with direct contact, that's how we're designed."*

Research Challenge: Find out what you can about Gina's take on working *with* nature, rather than against it. Ask yourself: what ten items would I take with me to survive alone in the wild?

CURTIS: THE GAMER WHO BECAME A SURFER, DANCER AND PARKOUR LEGEND

Curtis was 12 and spent his free time after school on his laptop, playing computer games. He and his mum had a great relationship, but they frequently argued about his screen time. For Curtis, being on the screen was fun and relaxing. It was a way to connect with friends, and it was all everyone spoke about at school.

In reality, Curtis was spending less face-to-face time with his friends. One day, some of his favourite people came for lunch, but Curtis's mum noticed him leave the table and disappear into his room. Perplexed, she followed him in, only to find him gaming again. It was time to reach a peace agreement.

'You don't get it. Gaming isn't the enemy here,' Curtis said.

'I do get it, you love it,' his mum responded

'Then why are you trying to stop me from doing something I love? You clearly don't care about who I am or what I enjoy!', Curtis shouted. His mum took a deep breath, fighting back the urge to deliver a gold-standard mini Tedtalk to him on sacrifice, love and gratitude. Instead, she said: 'I know you love gaming, but I also know you love your friends. And you love other things too, like skateboarding, surfing, parkour and tennis. But if all you do is game in your free time, then you won't get a chance to practise other skills. Connecting with people in real time is a skill that needs practice.'

Curtis listened, suppressing the instinct to roll his eyes. She had a point. He was finding social situations slightly harder. His mate had asked him to go surfing, but he made up an excuse about being sick because he hadn't been for ages and didn't want to make a fool of himself.

They both knew it was going to be hard, but, eventually, Curtis and his mum agreed that he could have time to play on his laptop after school on one condition: he had to do something physically active (and preferably outdoors) before he could have screen time. He also needed to communicate with his family before heading to his room.

Curtis was committed to honouring the promise he'd made to his mum and to himself. He started to play tennis, go surfing, attend lessons at a hip-hop class and visit the local parkour gym. Curtis noticed how much he was improving at sport and dance. He was connecting with new and old friends and becoming more confident. Curtis also realised he felt better because he was sleeping more.

It dawned on Curtis that while he had less time playing on his computer, he was enjoying his gaming time more. Curtis was doing more activities and yet he felt like he had more energy.

After three months of honouring the agreement with his mum, Curtis declared: 'From this moment on, I want to be living my life more and not be glued to a screen.'

Head to our Grow Your Mind website, click on the *How to be a Good Enough Kid* page and get a free copy of the activities.

And to practise some of the ideas from this chapter, check out the page opposite and the following two pages.

AWE HUNTING IDEAS:

Tick the places where you'd like to seek awe:

- ☐ Camp sites
- ☐ Hiking trails
- ☐ Beach
- ☐ Waterfalls
- ☐ Park
- ☐ Forest
- ☐ Under the sea
- ☐ Museum
- ☐ Planetarium
- ☐ Cave
- ☐ Large sports stadiums
- ☐ Libraries
- ☐ Garden
- ☐ Skyscrapers
- ☐ Aquariums

PRACTISE BEING A GOOD QUESTION ASKER

Tick the questions you might like to ask and add some of your own:

Can you tell me three things I don't know about you that might surprise me?

What would you do if you were stuck in a cave with no phone, water or light?

Where would you go right now if you could click your fingers and be there?

Why do you love [insert a thing, person or place] so much?

BEFORE YOU HIT THE SCREEN, HAVE YOU HAD SOME GREEN TIME?

Tick the ways you enjoy moving your body or being outside:

Kicking a footy
Shooting some hoops
Going for a run
Jumping in the water with a friend
Lying in the grass and looking at the clouds
Hugging at least four trees
Walking with your dog
Doing four cartwheels
Bushwalking
Riding your bike

PRACTISE BEING AN ONLINE DETECTIVE!

It's quite easy to be tricked online. You might be fooled by a news story that doesn't tell the truth or isn't based on facts. Maybe you get suckered in by a website which looks like a real business, but it's actually trying to steal your money or personal information. You might be misled by an image that doesn't tell the whole story; maybe it's been cropped or altered in some way to leave out important information. Maybe you're fooled by a person who is pretending to be someone else online. The eSafety Commissioner says there are things we can do to work out if an online source is fake. I want you to become fantastic at this exercise. Practise using these tips from the eSafety Commissioner next time something feels a little off online:

Maybe you are chatting to someone online and it feels uncomfortable or untrue. Use your Wise Owl to help you problem solve – are things not quite adding up? Tell a trusted adult.

Always double check information: maybe the story you're reading is fake. You can check it by looking for other stories on the subject. Are the facts repeated? Or do the stories sound wildly different?

Always check images. If you think an image or a video might be fake, you can search online and see if there are different versions of the same image.

Does something feel too good to be true? Maybe you get offered a prize? Chances are it's fake.

CHAPTER 10: HOW TO BE MORE OF A LEGEND

(READ THIS OUT LOUD USING YOUR BEST ANIMAL VOICES)

WHATEVER, LOOK AT SARA, SHE ISN'T PICKING UP RUBBISH
SHE PROBABLY DOESN'T WANT TO GET DIRTY BECAUSE SHE'S A GIRL
WHY WOULD BEING A GIRL STOP ME FROM GETTING DIRTY?
GIRLS LIKE TO BE CLEAN
GRRRR ENOUGH ALREADY. NOT COOL.
IT'S JUST A JOKE
WHAT ARE YOU LOOKING AT? GO BACK TO WHERE YOU CAME FROM.
BONDI?
BEFORE THAT
WHERE DID YOUR PARENTS COME FROM?
BEFORE WHAT?
DARWIN
THAT WAS ONLY A JOKE TOO!
GUYS?

HOW TO BE MORE OF A LEGEND

Have you ever hung out with someone who drained the life from you? They may have needed help to be more of a legend. And by legend, I don't mean saving lives and other unbelievable, heroic acts. Every single kid is good inside. I learned that from an authentic and helpful psychologist called Dr Becky Kennedy. This means even when you are rude or shout or scream, you are still good inside. Being a legend means that the good-inside part of you shines bright.

The characters in the comic were exasperated* by the non-rubbish picker-upper! To be fair, he was ticking all of the 'I am far from being a legend' boxes.

- ☐ **Complaining unnecessarily**
- ☐ **Name-calling**
- ☐ **Not helping**
- ☐ **Being sexist**
- ☐ **Being racist**

Being racist or sexist puts you in a whole other category of far-from-being-anywhere-near-a-legend. Words are powerful and cause harm. Even if you follow up your sexist or racist comment with a: 'Can't you take a joke?' or 'It was only a joke!' Those 'jokes' can make someone feel rubbish about themselves.

Remember, everyone is capable of changing into a legend. When a kid says something racist or sexist, they might not know that it's wrong or harmful. Maybe their family thinks it's okay. Maybe they saw something on their favourite show, or maybe they heard a YouTuber they admire say it. Or maybe, good enough kid, they were afraid of the unknown.

***Exasperated:**
To feel extremely annoyed.

We humans tend to lash out and make jokes at other people's expense if we're afraid. My generous assumption is that it's never too late to change and become more of a legend. Here are a few boxes to tick if you want to be a legend:

- ☐ **Be kind when no one is looking**
- ☐ **Congratulate a friend even though you wish you'd won**
- ☐ **Ask your parents how their day was**
- ☐ **Welcome the new kid into your game of dodgeball**

YOUR ANIMAL HELPERS FOR THIS CHAPTER

This chapter is about sharing some ways of you can stay or become more of a legend. And I don't mean heroic acts, I am sharing everyday small ways to choose helpfulness and kindness.

To be clear:

THE GOOD ENOUGH KID STILL COMPLAINS

Complaining is a normal part of being human. We should all be able to vent or share our thoughts and feelings. Like the boy in the comic strip, we also may have complained about picking up rubbish! Guess what, you can still complain and be a legend. Though there are times when complaining can lead you on a path to nowhere:

- Complaining constantly about things you just need to get on with
- Complaining with a whiny tone (use your normal voice – it's not nearly as grating).

HERE ARE SOME QUICK TIPS TO TRY BEFORE YOU COMPLAIN:

#1 TRY SWITCHING 'WHY ME?' TO 'WHY NOT ME?'

After all, why should it be someone else? This might sound silly, but it's helpful to remember we all must do things we don't like sometimes. We all have to do slightly annoying tasks. We all have things happen to us that are less than ideal. Why not you? Why should it be someone else?

#2 BEFORE COMPLAINING, BE CURIOUS

In fact, curiosity is the BIGGEST antidote to being no-where-near-a-legend. Being curious about complaining might sound like:

I wonder if complaining about this will make it easier for me?

I wonder why I want to complain? What is wrong about this?

I wonder what a fairer outcome would look like?

I wonder if there is an interesting way to look at this task?

I wonder if complaining the whole time will affect how I see this experience?

I wonder if I will need to do this thing whether I complain or not?

I repeat: I'm not suggesting you shouldn't get help when you need it. I'm not saying you shouldn't talk about your problems with someone you trust. You should never feel alone with your feelings. But we need to work out the fine balance between processing feelings and complaining. If you are complaining, there is probably a problem. But can you solve it without complaining? Learn how to be a problem solver by using the steps in this flow chart.

ARE YOU READY TO BE A PROBLEM SOLVER?

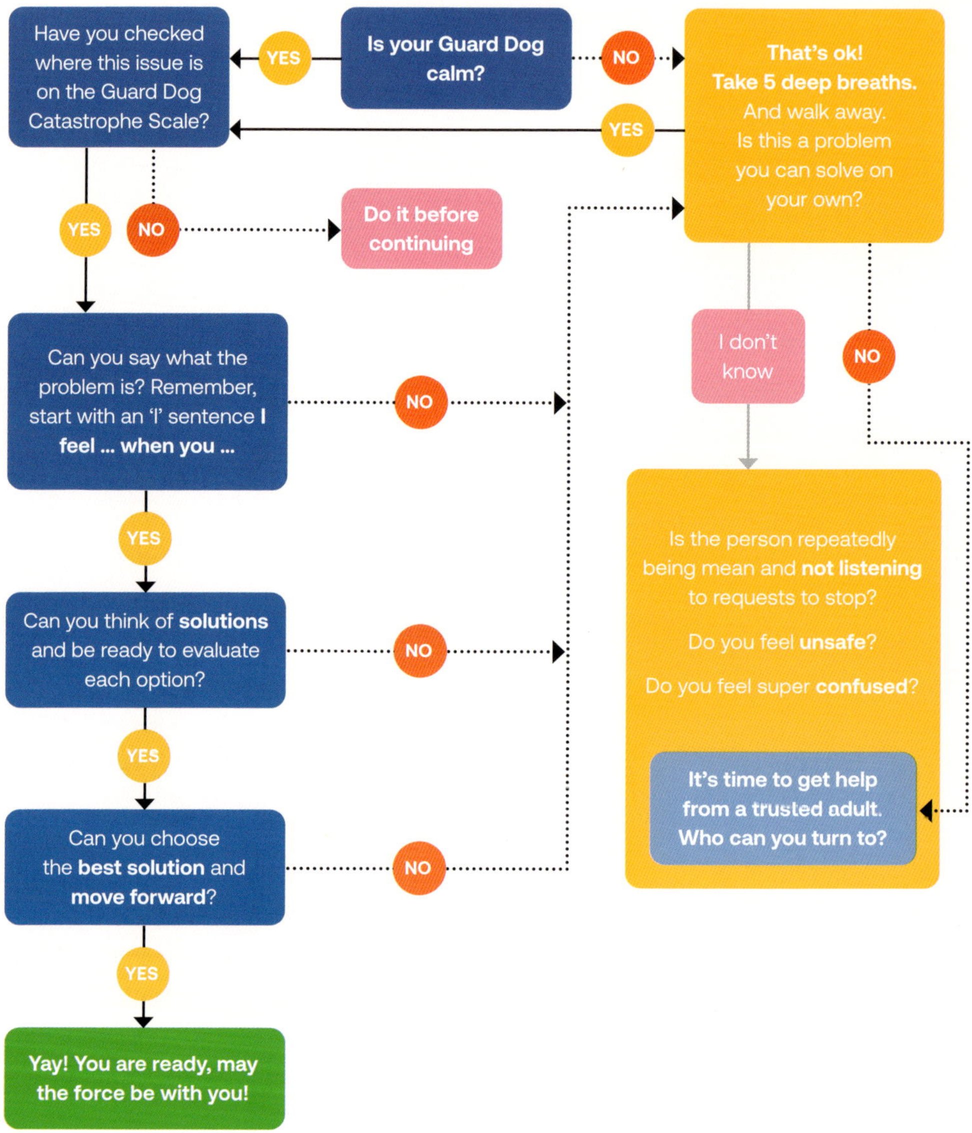

#3 GRATITUDE IS PRETTY MUCH THE OPPOSITE OF COMPLAINING

Try replacing 'have to' with 'get to':

I have to go to soccer practice
→ **I get to go to soccer practice**

I have to take my dog for a walk
→ **I get to take my dog for a walk**

Okay. Now a few tips on being more of a legend.

BE OF BENEFIT (B.O.B)

A brilliant example of someone who has lived by the 'Be of Benefit' mindset is Jane Goodall, certified legend. Jane is famous for her work saving chimpanzees from extinction due to hunting. The first step to being a legend is to listen to her take on the impact we all have on the world. She says:

> YOU CANNOT GET THROUGH A SINGLE DAY WITHOUT HAVING AN IMPACT ON THE WORLD AROUND YOU. WHAT YOU DO MAKES A DIFFERENCE, AND YOU HAVE TO DECIDE WHAT KIND OF DIFFERENCE YOU WANT TO MAKE.

B.O.B means we use our character strengths not only to help ourselves, but to help those around us. It's a mindset – a frame of mind, an attitude and an approach to life. A big-hearted educator and researcher called Ash Buchanan coined the term 'benefit mindset'.

FIXED MINDSET	GROWTH MINDSET	BENEFIT MINDSET
You believe your intelligence is fixed.	You believe you can grow and improve by effort.	You believe in your ability to help others and why this is important.
Mistakes are something to be avoided.	Mistakes are a key part of learning.	You help to create positive change.

Helping others is the best way to help yourself. We feel better when we switch our focus from 'me' to 'we' (cheers, Sifting Sooty). Our other animals can help us remember to be helpful (thanks, Elephant), they can help us make a good choice (cheers, Wise Owl), they can remind us it's not a threat when someone asks us to complete a chore at home (thanks, Guard Dog) and they can imagine how others will feel if we B.O.B it up (gracias, Octopus).

A BENEFIT MINDSET AT SCHOOL MIGHT LOOK LIKE:

- Offering to carry something for a teacher
- Picking up rubbish, even if it's not yours

A BENEFIT MINDSET AT HOME MIGHT LOOK LIKE:

- Helping with household chores without complaining

A BENEFIT MINDSET TO THE PLANET MIGHT LOOK LIKE:

- Packing a waste-free lunch

Spreading the idea that being of benefit is a good thing. The more people help others, the better. And speaking of spreading things, here are a few things that are also contagious:

- A cold
- Kindness

Kindness is how we act and treat others, but what's this? It's contagious? Yep, in the same way you might catch a cold if I sneeze on you, you will also catch my kindness. Have you heard about the ripple effect?

When we do something kind, others may notice and feel inspired to be kind themselves. The person who received the kindness may also feel a greater desire to be kind to others.

The Wild Robot

LEGENDS CHOOSE TO BE KINDER THAN NECESSARY

Kindness = being a legend
Kinder than necessary = being a massive legend

What does it mean to be kinder than necessary? For me, it means you don't hesitate; you're the first to say 'hi', you're the first to include people, you're the first to stand up for a friend. You're kind even when no one is looking and you may never be rewarded for it.

You really need help from all your animals to be kinder than necessary. It's hard to be kind when your Guard Dog is barking, warning you of every possible threat. It's hard to be kind when your Sifting Sooty is fixated on your flaws. It's hard to be kind if you don't ask your Sensitive Octopus to imagine how it might feel for someone else to receive your kindness. It's near impossible to be kind if your Elephant is sleep-deprived and you've forgotten that you like to be kind.

YOU AREN'T SUPPOSED TO HAVE FAVOURITES, BUT ...

My favourite form of kindness to offer (and to receive) is to feel seen. Sometimes I watch my kids arrive at sports practice and no one says 'hi' to them. Saying 'hi' first is totally an act of kindness. It's brave, because you may not get a 'hi' back. But I believe it's worth it to prevent, for example, a new kid feeling invisible.

KINDNESS IS HAVING AWKWARD CONVERSATIONS

You might tell your friend they have food on their face. You might have to explain that you don't like it when they talk over you or link arms with you. It's unkind to not let someone know when they're bothering you.

Clear is kind.

Tact* helps when you're telling the truth.

***Tact**

Telling the truth in a way that's kind and polite. For example, someone serves you pasta and you yell: 'I HATE PASTA!' A tactful way to express yourself might be: 'Thank you for the food, I'm not mad about pasta.'

IS IT KINDNESS OR SOMETHING ELSE?

Before you act, engage your Sensitive Octopus; consider how the person receiving the kindness will feel. Here's an example:

You rock up to play basketball and there's a new kid in a wheelchair who wants to play. She says she's played all her life and loves it. She joins in, but every time she gets the ball everyone hangs back, nervous to hurt her. They think they're being kind, but they have missed a key requirement of kindness: considering the feelings of others. She leaves the game upset. Why? Because she wants to play properly and be treated equally; she wants to belong.

WE SHOULD ALSO BE KIND TO OURSELVES

The way we talk to ourselves matters. The words we say to ourselves can look like self-compassion or self-sabotage*. We can also be kind or cruel to our bodies.

<u>*Self-sabotage</u>

This is when people get in the way of their own success. For example, if you speak to yourself in an unkind way, you might believe those negative thoughts, which stops you from succeeding.

You can practise kindness to yourself and others with something called a 'loving kindness meditation':

Close or soften your eyes and think to yourself:
May I be healthy, may I be strong, I wish myself well.

When we are kind to ourselves, we are more likely to be kind to others too. Another act of self-kindness is making time for joy and doing the things you love. If you love cooking, painting or singing – make time! Remember what we learned in Chapter 9 – get your DOSE of wellbeing!

RECEIVE KINDNESS

Good enough kid, it's super important to receive kindness because it's actually a kind thing to do! According to some studies, when you receive kindness from someone you're helping them live longer!

Kindness is the best way to be a legend. There are other ways too.

LEGENDS DON'T HAVE TO BE THE SMARTEST PERSON IN THE ROOM

Adults who think they're the smartest are slightly grating to be around. Being a legend means you ask good questions and are always open to learning something new. It also means you can admit when you're wrong. It feels rubbish, but it is more rubbish when you never admit fault. People will stop trusting you if you don't acknowledge your mistakes. If you make a mistake, call on your Guard Dog to help you. It can ask: 'Is admitting I'm wrong a threat, challenge or opportunity?'

LEGENDS CAN HANDLE REJECTION

As you enter your teenage years and adulthood, you might start dating. People will break up with you and some people will not fancy you. But because you're a legend, you respect other people's right to live their lives. Knowing you're a good enough person (which you are) will help you be resilient to rejection.

LEGENDS DON'T THINK THEY'RE BETTER THAN EVERYONE ELSE

Your gender, age, sexuality, religion, how much money you have or where you come from doesn't make you more important than anyone else. Obviously, we want to feel good about ourselves; we want to be confident and have self-worth. But there is a difference between valuing ourselves and believing we are above others. That's why this book is not called: *How to be an awesome, sensational kid*.

LEGENDS DON'T LAUGH AT DISCRIMINATORY COMMENTS

Words hurt – especially when they mock someone's race, gender, ability, sexuality, age or religion. Just because someone says something is a joke, doesn't mean you have to feel like a bore for not laughing.

Words can be dangerous. Research shows that gender inequality drives gendered violence. If you're the person making the sexist joke, you might feel funny, cool and popular because people laugh. And if you're the one laughing, it signals to other people that it's okay to be sexist. This is one of the many reasons why gender inequality still exists. When we laugh at these jokes, we add to a problem instead of being part of the solution. When you hear a discriminatory joke, do not add fuel to the fire. Be a legend, and simply say: 'That's not funny.'

LEGENDS MAKE AMENDS

You will stuff up and hurt people. It's a part of life. Being a total legend means you apologise and repair the hurt you've caused. You *choose* kindness. It's a choice. **So, choose it!**

SHINE THE SPOTLIGHT ON ...

KATH KOSCHEL:

SPEAKER, SURVIVOR + SPREADER OF KINDNESS

"You don't go through what I have, overcome it and live to tell the story without receiving a lot of kindness ... and I guess it's my job now to propel that mission and that message."

Research Challenge: Look up Kath Koschel and the Kindness Factory. What did you learn? How do you think kindness might help yourself and others in tricky times?

Kindness is a gift; it's most powerful and authentic in everyday, small ways. When we hear about grand gestures, we can sometimes feel small and unable to match them. But here are some examples of kindness which prove we're ALL capable of choosing to be kind:

Henry was obsessed with sport and lunch times. His mate broke his leg, so Henry chose to stay in during each break to keep him company.

Mila always sat in a horseshoe formation. She kept her group open for others to join. She used her popularity for good, making others feel seen and included. She always defended the underdog.

Clementine was forever cheering on her soccer team, making new team members feel comfortable and reassuring players when they missed a shot or a pass.

Rohan noticed his friend with cerebral palsy could not reach the pens. He quietly passed them to him without any fuss or need for recognition.

Banjo rocked up to a school disco with a pocket of gold coins. He proceeded to buy bags of sweets for his friends who had forgotten their money.

Jessie wrote a note to the new kid which said: 'Welcome, you can ask me questions any time.'

Brishti quietly helped her friend who was struggling with a maths problem. She was super patient and encouraging.

Atticus arrived at a party. He noticed his sister was distressed about forgetting her shoes, so he promptly took his off and left them at the front door so they would both be barefoot.

BRAIN BREAK:

What animal am I?

When I feel threatened, I squirt out toxic venom that can break down flesh. I will aim for your eyes, and if you don't wash out my venom quickly it will load to severe pain and possible blindness.

This is the final Practice Makes Progress section. I really hope you feel good enough by now. I hope you're ready to spread curiosity and kindness around your home and school like a virulent gastro bug. You've got this, legend.

Listen to Grow Your Mind podcast episodes:

B.O.B It Up
Ghosting
Your Future Self Will Thank You
It's Contagious

Also, head to our website, click on the *How to be a Good Enough Kid* page and get a free copy of the activities.

And to practise some of the ideas from this chapter, try the different kindness challenges on the page opposite every day for a week.

Monday: Kindness is SUPER good for others and for our own mental health. Have you heard about random acts of kindness? At Grow Your Mind we like this idea, but we much prefer being kind on purpose. So – make a plan right now. Who can you be kind to today? How will you do it?

Tuesday: Put names in a hat for every person in your house; consider including some of your neighbours. Draw out a name. Write down three kind things about this person. Leave the list in your neighbour's letterbox or outside a family member's bedroom door.

Wednesday: It's easier to be kind to others when we're kind to ourselves. What is one nice thing you can do for yourself today?

Thursday: Reflect on an act of kindness you received. What happened and how did it make you feel? Who can you help feel this way today?

Friday: A form of kindness is generosity. How can you be generous this weekend?

A FINAL WORD BEFORE YOU GO FORTH, YOU EVEN BIGGER LEGEND

So, legends, now you know what a good enough kid is: it's you. You are good inside; everyone is. If you keep up your mental fitness, that good-inside stuff will shine out of you like a full moon on a remote beach. Remember, your brain is there to help you; you can work with it to thrive. You can wake up your Sifting Sooty and get it to focus on all the good things around you by mindfully breathing and tapping into your senses. You can help your Sensitive Octopus reach its full potential by showing kindness to others, imagining another person's perspective and being willing to change your mind. You can unleash the benefits of good decision-making by taking some mindful breaths to strengthen your Wise Owl. You can rock your ability to learn and remember things by getting enough sleep and moving your body every single day, helping that Elephant of yours feel good. And you can be brave in uncomfortable situations by asking your Guard Dog: is this a threat, a challenge or an opportunity?

Please, go forth and try some of the tips and techniques in this book because, really, you can't fail. Why? Because practice makes ... (I don't even need to finish that sentence, do I?). If you drop the ball on generous assumptions, if you sink into worrying that you never win and you don't have enough, if you find yourself losing your cool a lot – pause and come back to what brings you joy. And be sure to have self-compassion; you are doing the best you can – we all are, and you are *absolutely* good enough.

ACKNOWLEDGMENTS

This book was a team effort. Yes, my name is on it but as the ultra-cheesy saying goes: There is no 'i' in team.

And my word do I have an incredible team. I get to work with the brightest, funniest, kindest and most creative people you could imagine. A huge shout out to my dear friend, snorkelling companion and co-founder, Kristina (Tina) Freeman. Tina is the epitome of love and vulnerability, she oozes thoughtfulness and warmth. There would be no Grow Your Mind without her.

Other contributors to this book to whom I am indebted to are Jules, Lizzy, Annabelle, Nat, Lisa, Becky, Chardie, Nicky and the Lucys in my life, they are all dear friends and talented humans.

A massive thank you to all of the inspiring people who work in the field of wellbeing science. This book has drawn on hundreds of researchers and thought leaders.

To NewSouth Publishing and my clever and witty copyeditor, Kelly Frame, thank you for guiding me through my first book with patience and humour!

Thanks to the talented and clever Beck Feiner for her vibrant and striking illustrations.

And to my wise, exceedingly kind and wonderful husband, Andy, and my three delightful, loving and curious children, Clementine, Atticus and Banjo: Thank you for a life predominantly filled with joy, awe and glimmer-seeking. Don't go changing punks.

ANSWERS TO BRAIN BREAK QUESTIONS

CHAPTER 1

What animal am I?

I have three hearts, I can regrow lost arms and I've been around for about 296 million years. I can pull the arms off a crab and inject it with a paralysis venom which causes the crab's enzymes to dissolve its own muscles, then I suck the crab meat out like a milkshake.

OCTOPUS

CHAPTER 2

What animal am I?

I have super skinny legs and people think I'm the most venomous spider. People also think I can't bite humans because my fangs are too small. The truth is, I *can* bite people, but I'm not deadly at all.

DADDY-LONG-LEGS

CHAPTER 3

What living thing am I?

I'm so small you can only see me with the help of a microscope. I help you digest food and I tune up your immune system. There are millions of me in your body. I'm found in food too.

MICROBES

CHAPTER 4

What animal am I?

I have 'Pink Fairy' at the start of my name. I know, it's tough to be taken seriously. The other part of my name in Spanish means 'little armoured one'. I'm tiny and a proud tunneller, which means I live underground. I have soft fur, a tail and relatively large feet.

PINK FAIRY ARMADILLO

CHAPTER 5

What is this invertebrate?

It aerates and mixes the soil, making it richer in nutrients. Charles Darwin (who studied nature and came up with a theory of evolution) once wrote about this ear-less creature: 'It may be doubted whether there are many other animals which have played so important a part in the history of the world, as have these lowly organised creatures.'

EARTHWORMS

CHAPTER 6

What animal am I?

I'm one of the most venomous animals in the world. My head is the size of a golf ball. You will know when I'm in threat mode as my blue rings will appear and start to pulsate! Run for your life when this happens as I pack enough venom to kill 25 humans.

BLUE-RINGED OCTOPUS

CHAPTER 7

What animal am I?

I evolved over 420 million years ago. That means I am 200 million years older than dinosaurs. My skeleton is cartilage (the same thing your nose and ears are made of).

SHARK

CHAPTER 8

What animal am I?

I survive on a diet of highly toxic eucalyptus leaves, but my digestive system is equipped with a special bacterium to digest these otherwise deadly greens. I am outrageously cute, but I can also be ruthless.

KOALA

CHAPTER 9

What animal am I?

When biologists first found me (dead) they sent me to London from Australia and people thought it was a HOAX. Someone had clearly killed a duck and stuck its poor beak onto the body of another fluffy animal with strange, webbed feet. They were wrong. I'm very shy, I have a beautiful coat like an otter, webbed toes and a soft leathery bill.

PLATYPUS

CHAPTER 10

What animal am I?

When I feel threatened, I squirt out toxic venom that can break down flesh. I will aim for your eyes, and if you don't wash out my venom quickly it will lead to severe pain and possible blindness.

GIANT SPITTING COBRA

A NewSouth book

Published by
NewSouth Publishing
University of New South Wales Press Ltd
University of New South Wales
Sydney NSW 2052
AUSTRALIA
https://unsw.press/

First published 2025

10 9 8 7 6 5 4 3 2

ISBN:
9781761170188 (paperback)
9781761178252 (ePDF)

A catalogue record for this book is available from the National Library of Australia

Design and typesetting Alissa Dinallo
Illustrations Beck Feiner
Printer Everbest, China

This book is printed on paper using fibre supplied from plantation or sustainably managed forests.

UNSW
SYDNEY